THE PSALMS

A JOURNAL

THE PSALMS
A JOURNAL

Kenneth Boa

NAVPRESS
BRINGING TRUTH TO LIFE
P.O. Box 35001, Colorado Springs, Colorado 80935

OUR GUARANTEE TO YOU

We believe so strongly in the message of our books that we are making this quality guarantee to you. If for any reason you are disappointed with the content of this book, return the title page to us with your name and address and we will refund to you the list price of the book. To help us serve you better, please briefly describe why you were disappointed. Mail your refund request to: NavPress, P.O. Box 35002, Colorado Springs, CO 80935.

The Navigators is an international Christian organization. Our mission is to reach, disciple, and equip people to know Christ and to make Him known through successive generations. We envision multitudes of diverse people in the United States and every other nation who have a passionate love for Christ, live a lifestyle of sharing Christ's love, and multiply spiritual laborers among those without Christ.

NavPress is the publishing ministry of The Navigators. NavPress publications help believers learn biblical truth and apply what they learn to their lives and ministries. Our mission is to stimulate spiritual formation among our readers.

The introductory material in this journal was adapted from the section on devotional spirituality in Kenneth Boa's book, *Conformed to His Image* (Grand Rapids: Zondervan Publishing House, 2001), with permission of the publishers.

© 2001 by Kenneth Boa
All rights reserved. No part of this publication may be reproduced in any form without written permission from NavPress, P.O. Box 35001, Colorado Springs, CO 80935.
www.navpress.com
Library of Congress Catalog Card Number: 00-030517
ISBN 1-57683-251-1

Cover design by Dan Jamison
Cover calligraphy by Don Bishop/Artville
Cover photo by PhotoDisc
Creative team: Jacqueline Eaton Blakley, Lori Mitchell, Glynese Northam

Boa, Kenneth.
        The psalms : a journal : spiritual formation through personal encounters with scripture / Kenneth Boa.
        p. cm.
        ISBN 1-57683-251-1
        1. Bible. O.T. Psalms—Devotional literature. 2. Spiritual journals—Authorship.
I. Title.

BS1430.4 .B57 2001
248.3—dc21

                                                                00-030517

Printed in the United States of America

1 2 3 4 5 6 7 8 9 10 / 05 04 03 02 01

FOR A FREE CATALOG OF
NAVPRESS BOOKS & BIBLE STUDIES,
CALL 1-800-366-7788 (USA)
OR 1-416-499-4615 (CANADA)

Inside This Journal

AN INTRODUCTION
TO THE PSALMS

OUR IMAGE OF GOD

> *There is but one God, the Father, from whom are all things, and*
> *we exist for Him; and one Lord, Jesus Christ, by whom are all*
> *things, and we exist through Him.*
>
> —1 Corinthians 8:6

We do not exist for ourselves—we exist *for* the Father and *through* the Son. The world tells us that we derive our existence from it and that we should live for ourselves, but the Word teaches us that all we are and have comes from the Father who formed us for His pleasure and purposes.

Ultimate reality is not the cosmos or a mysterious force, but an infinite and loving Person. The implications of this are astounding and pervasive. The infinite-personal Lord of all is an unbounded loving community of three timeless and perfect Persons. In the superabundance of His joy and life, He is at once solitude and society, the one and the many, supernal being as communion. The magnificent God who abounds in personal plenitude has no needs, yet He invites us to participate in the intense and interpenetrating life of the three eternally subsistent Selves. Jesus prayed on our behalf "that they may all be one; even as You, Father, are in Me and I in You, that they also may be in Us. . . . I in them and You in Me, that they may be perfected in unity, so that the world may know that You sent Me, and loved them, even as You have loved Me" (John 17:21,23). The impenetrable mystery of us being in the divine Us, and the divine Us being in us, transcends our imagination—but if it is true, all else pales in comparison.

Devotional spirituality revels in the glorious attributes of God and aspires to lay hold of God's aspiration for us. It prepares our souls for the "mystic sweet communion" of living entirely in God and in one another as the three Persons of God eternally live and rejoice in one another. It instills in us a passion for Christ's indwelling life and inspires us to swim in the river of torrential love that flows from His throne of grace.

In 1677, Henry Scougal observed in his little book *The Life of God in the Soul of Man,* that "The worth and excellency of a soul is to be measured by the object of its love." Our souls become emaciated when their pleasure is affixed to position, possessions, and power, because these things are destined to corrupt and perish. But as we gradually (and often painfully) transfer our affections from the created and finite world to the uncreated and infinite Maker of the world, our souls become great and glorious. As we take the risk of seeking God's pleasure above our own, we discover the ironic byproduct of a greater satisfaction and contentment than if we sought these things as ends in themselves. As we learn to fix our eyes on Jesus, not for His benefits but *for Himself,* we find that we have all things in Him.

Scripture teaches us that we steadily become conformed to what we most love and admire. *We become like our focus;* as we behold the glory of the Lord, we are being "transformed into the same image from glory to glory, just as from the Lord, the Spirit" (2 Corinthians 3:18). We gradually come to resemble what we worship. But if our heart's desire is fixed on something in this world, it becomes idolatrous and soul-corrupting. Hosea declared that the people of Israel "became as detestable as that which they loved" (Hosea 9:10). But when we turn the focus of our love away from the idols of this world system to the beauty of Christ, we discover the liberty of the Spirit of the Lord. If we draw life from loving communion with the caring, radiant, majestic, and unfathomable Being who formed us for Himself, our souls become noble as they grow in conformity to His character.

GOD'S WORLD, HIS WORD, HIS WORKS, AND HIS WAYS

God in His inner essence is a mystery beyond our comprehension; we will never know Him as He knows Himself. The great pilgrims along the way have discovered that progress from superficial to substantive apprehension of God is not so much a movement from darkness to light as it is a plummeting into the ever-increasing profundity of the cloud of unknowing. Kallistos Ware in *The Orthodox Way* distinguishes the *essence* of God and the *energies* of God. In His essence, God is radically transcendent, but in His energies, He is immanent and omnipresent. As Ware notes, "The Godhead is simple and indivisible, and has no parts. The essence signifies the whole God as he is in himself; the energies signify the whole God as he is in action. God in His entirety is completely present in each of his divine energies." As we reflect on the way God reveals Himself, we come to know Him more clearly, and this enables us to love Him more dearly, and to follow Him more nearly. God makes Himself known to us through His world, His Word, His works, and His ways.

Loving God Through His World

> *The heavens are telling of the glory of God; and their expanse is declaring the work of His hands.*
>
> —Psalm 19:1

> *O Lord, how many are Your works! In wisdom You have made them all; the earth is full of Your possessions.*
>
> —Psalm 104:24

8

Read Psalm 19:1-6 and Psalms 104 and 148 carefully and prayerfully, and you will be struck by the manifold ways in which God designed the heavens and earth to display His glory, wisdom, and greatness.

Meditation on the created order is too often neglected as a meaningful component of devotional spirituality. This is unfortunate, because creation abounds with resplendent wonders on every order of magnitude from the microcosm to the macrocosm that point beyond themselves to the beauty and unimaginable brilliance of the Creator of the cosmos. Consider these marvels of order and design: particles and atoms, light and colors, microbes and diatoms, snowflakes, insects, seeds, flowers, leaves, shells, rocks and minerals, fruits, vegetables, plants, small and large birds, small and large fish, whales, small and large animals, trees, mountains, clouds, weather, the seasons, our earth, the planets, stars, nebulae, our galaxy, clusters and super-clusters of galaxies.

You formed my inward parts; You wove me in my mother's womb.
I will give thanks to You, for I am fearfully and wonderfully
made; wonderful are Your works, and my soul knows it very well.
—Psalm 139:13-14

Of all God's created works, the human body best displays God's creative skill and design. I recommend two books that will help you worship God by reflecting on the marvels of the human and spiritual body: *Fearfully and Wonderfully Made* and *In His Image* by Dr. Paul Brand and Philip Yancey. These books portray the way physical systems like cells, bone, skin, motion, blood, the head, and the sensation of pain teach spiritual truth.

Let me mention two things that have helped me love God through His world. The first is an occasional trip to special places where I am encompassed in the natural order. In such places I sometimes sit back and stare at the stars until I realize that I am no longer looking up, but also *down,* and that I am wholly enveloped by the splendor and grandeur of the heavens. An experience like this is humbling because it dramatically shifts my perspective and reminds me that apart from God and His grace, I am nothing. I gain a similar sense of awe by looking at recent photographs of star clouds and distant galaxies. The veritable explosion in scientific knowledge in our time gives us access to new avenues of appreciating God that were never before available.

The second thing I use to stimulate wonder is a set of field lenses and a miniature high-intensity flashlight. I use this "nature kit" from time to time to observe otherwise invisible colors and patterns in flowers, insects, rocks, and so forth. The very act of slowing down enough to observe and appreciate the rich intricacy and diversity of the created order is a healthy exercise in recollection and renewal.

There is no limit to the images and insights that can be gleaned from nature if we take the time and have the eyes to see. We would do well to cultivate a childlike sense of amazement and awe at the things we tend to overlook every day. Our artificial environments and busy schedules make us forget that we are surrounded by mystery and majesty. I encourage you to make the effort to enjoy more frequent and deliberate contact with God's creation and to develop a deeper appreciation for the complexity, beauty, and resplendence of the heavens and the earth. As you do this, you will sense that the God who designed all this and spoke it into being is utterly competent, trustworthy, and lovable.

Loving God Through His Word

Open my eyes, that I may behold wonderful things from Your law.
—Psalm 119:18

The Word of God restores the soul, imparts wisdom, gives joy to the heart, enlightens the eyes, reveals God's righteousness, and endures forever.
—Psalm 19:7-9

Scripture was revealed not merely to inform us, but to transform us. In *Shaped by the Word*, M. Robert Mulholland Jr. contrasts two approaches to Scripture:

INFORMATIONAL READING	FORMATIONAL READING
Seeks to cover as much as possible	Focuses on small portions
A linear process	An in-depth process
Seeks to master the text	Allows the text to master us
The text as an object to use	The text as a subject that shapes us
Analytical, critical, and judgmental approach	Humble, detached, willing, loving approach
Problem-solving mentality	Openness to mystery

There is an important place for informational reading of Scripture and for exegetical and topical methods of Bible study. But those who approach Scripture only in this way often overlook the formational approach that centers on speaking to the heart more than informing the mind. The Bible is not merely an object, but a divinely inspired oracle that is "living and active"

(Hebrews 4:12) and has the power to transform those who receive it in humility and obedience (James 1:21-22). Devotional spirituality stresses the formative power of revealed truth and encourages us to love God through His Word. We will look at a time-tested method of doing this in the pages ahead.

Loving God Through His Works

Say to God, "How awesome are Your works!"
Come and see the works of God,
Who is awesome in His deeds toward the sons of men.
I shall remember the deeds of the Lord;
Surely I will remember Your wonders of old.
I will meditate on all Your work
And muse on Your deeds.
You are the God who works wonders;
You have made known Your strength among the peoples.
You have by Your power redeemed Your people.

—Psalms 66:3,5; 77:11-12,14-15

The psalmists frequently reviewed and reflected upon God's historical acts of redemption, protection, and provision. Both Testaments abound with accounts of how God has worked in specific and dramatic ways in the lives of people and in the destiny of nations. He has demonstrated His just and loving purposes in the arena of human history, and prayerful consideration of His mighty works of creation, redemption, and consummation is another way of enhancing our worship and devotion for the triune Godhead.

Worthy are You, our Lord and our God, to receive glory and
honor and power; for You created all things, and because of Your
will they existed, and were created. . . . Worthy are You to take
the book and to break its seals; for You were slain, and purchased
for God with Your blood men from every tribe and tongue and
people and nation. You have made them to be a kingdom and
priests to our God; and they will reign upon the earth. . . . Wor-
thy is the Lamb that was slain to receive power and riches and
wisdom and might and honor and glory and blessing. . . . To Him
who sits on the throne, and to the Lamb, be blessing and honor
and glory and dominion forever and ever.

—Revelation 4:11; 5:9-10,12-13

Loving God Through His Ways

He made known His ways to Moses, His acts to the sons of Israel.

—Psalm 103:7

11

Moses not only knew the Lord through His works, but he also knew and loved the Lord through His ways. God's ways concern His personal involvement in our lives and our experience of His peace, power, provision, protection, compassion, and care. It is good to build a "personal history" of God's providential care by reviewing and remembering the things He has done at various points along your spiritual journey. Remember His surprising answers to prayer, the way He drew you to Himself, the way He carried you through turbulent waters, the way He provided for your needs when circumstances looked hopeless, the way He encouraged and comforted you in your distress, the way He exhorted you through others and disciplined you for your good, and the way He seeks to strip you of your hope in the things of this world so that you will learn to hope only in Him.

> *Come and hear, all who fear God,*
> *And I will tell of what He has done for my soul.*
> *Certainly God has heard;*
> *He has given heed to the voice of my prayer.*
> *Blessed be God,*
> *Who has not turned away my prayer*
> *Nor His lovingkindness from me.*
> *Your way, O God, is holy;*
> *What god is great like our God?*
>
> —Psalm 66:16,19-20; 77:13

I will tell of what He has done for my soul. Grateful reflection on what God has done for your soul is a vital component of devotional spirituality.

God's ways also relate to the multifaceted attributes of His person, powers, and perfection. Because our capacity to love God is related to our image of God, we do well to pray for the grace of growing in understanding of the glories of His attributes: His unlimited power, presence, and knowledge; His holiness, justice, goodness, truthfulness, and righteousness; His goodness, grace, compassion, mercy, and love; His beauty, glory, greatness, transcendent majesty, and dominion; and His self-existence, eternity, infinity, and immutability. As Dallas Willard puts it in *The Divine Conspiracy,* God is "an interlocking community of magnificent persons, completely self-sufficing and with no meaningful limits on goodness and power." He is the absolute answer to the perennial quest for the true, the good, and the beautiful.

THE PRACTICE OF SACRED READING

The ancient art of sacred reading *(lectio divina)* centers on loving God through His Word. It was introduced to the West by the Eastern desert father John Cassian early in the fifth century. The sixth-century Rule of St. Benedict that guided Benedictine and Cistercian monastic practice prescribed daily periods for sacred reading. Unfortunately, by the end of the Middle Ages it came to be seen as a method that should be restricted to the spiritually elite. As time passed, even monastics lost the simplicity of sacred reading as it was replaced by more complicated systems and forms of "mental prayer." In recent decades, however, this ancient practice has been revitalized, especially by those in the Cistercian tradition. Writers like Thomas Merton (*Contemplative Prayer, New Seeds of Contemplation, Spiritual Direction & Meditation*), Thomas Keating (*Open Mind, Open Heart*), Michael Casey (*Sacred Reading, Toward God, The Undivided Heart*), and Thelma Hall (*Too Deep for Words*) have been promoting sacred reading in Catholic circles, and Protestants are now being exposed to this approach as well. Sacred reading, or *lectio divina*, involves a progression through the four movements of reading, meditation, prayer, and contemplation.

READING (LECTIO)

In his study of monastic culture, *The Love of Learning and the Desire for God*, Jean Leclercq distinguished two distinct approaches to Scripture that were used in the Middle Ages. While medieval universities were urban schools that prepared clerics for the active life, rural monasteries focused on spiritual formation within a liturgical framework to equip monks for the contemplative life. The scholastics approached Scripture by focusing on the page of sacred text (*sacra pagina*) as an object to be studied and investigated by putting questions to the text (*quaestio*) and by questioning oneself with the subject matter (*disputatio*). By contrast, the monastics approached Scripture through a personal orientation of meditation (*meditatio*) and prayer (*oratio*). While the scholastics sought science and knowledge in the text, the monastics sought wisdom and appreciation. Those in the schools were more oriented to the objective, the theological, and the cognitive; those in the cloisters were more oriented to the subjective, the devotional, and the affective.

Most contemporary approaches to Bible study have more in common with the scholastics than with the monastics. Recalling a distinction we made earlier, they are more concerned with informational reading than with formational reading. There is a legitimate need for both approaches, since an overemphasis on one or the other can lead to the extremes of cold intellectualism or mindless enthusiasm. But when evangelicals study Scripture, they typically look more for precepts and principles than for an encounter with God in the depths of their being. The practice of *lectio divina* can correct this lack of balance, because it stresses the reading of Scripture for spiritual formation through receptive openness to God's loving call of grace. *Lectio* is not an intellectual exercise that seeks to control and to gather information, but a voluntary immersion in the Word of God that seeks to receive and to respond. Spiritual reading melds revelation with experience. It is done in the spirit of the collect for the second Sunday in Advent in the 1928 *Book of Common Prayer:*

Blessed Lord, who hast caused all holy Scriptures to be written for our learning; Grant that we may in such wise hear them, read, mark, learn, and inwardly digest them, that by patience and comfort of thy holy Word, we may embrace, and ever hold fast, the blessed hope of everlasting life, which thou hast given us in our Saviour Jesus Christ.

May we learn to hear the holy Scriptures and to "read, mark, learn, and inwardly digest" them.

Suggestions for Reading

- Choose a special place (preferably away from your desk and other areas of activity) that is suitable for this purpose. Sanctify this space by reserving it as a regular meeting place with the Lord.
- Choose a special time in which you can be alert and consistent. Invite God to lead you to rearrange your life to allow more time with Him. This will be more a matter of making time rather than finding time. Making time for this purpose is a response to God's calling in a world of constant external demands. Although this will not work for everyone, I recommend exchanging the last hour of the night for an extra hour in the morning. (Most of us could redeem a significant amount of time by reducing and being more selective in our intake of television.) Whenever it is, give God your best time, when you are least sluggish, and when you can be quiet, still, and unpressured by outward hindrances.
- Consistency is critical, since there will be many temptations to postpone and neglect sacred reading. The benefits of *lectio* are attained gradually over a long-term process.
- Because *lectio divina* engages the whole person, your bodily posture is important. A seated position that is erect but not tense or slouched is best for the four movements of *lectio*. It is good to be fully attentive and alert without sitting in a way that will eventually impede your circulation or breathing.
- Try to be systematic in the way you select your Scripture texts. They can emerge from a daily Bible reading program or through the use of a lectionary that gives you daily Old Testament, gospel, and epistle readings. Or your passages can come out of a devotional guide. (I often use my *Handbook to Prayer* and *Handbook to Renewal* for this purpose.)
- To avoid distraction in sacred reading, it is better to use a Bible without study notes. Use an accurate translation rather than a paraphrase (I use the updated edition of the NASB) for *lectio divina*.
- Keep the passage brief—do not confuse quantity with quality.
- It is also helpful to apply this method of slow, deliberate, and prayerful reading to other resources such as the creeds, traditional and patristic texts, and classic spiritual books. Samples of some of these resources are

available in *Devotional Classics,* edited by Richard J. Foster and James Bryan Smith. Older literature has a way of challenging the biases of our modern presuppositions, if we will let it seep into us.

- Begin with a prayer of preparation: for example, "Open my eyes, that I may behold wonderful things from Your law" (Psalm 119:18), or "Let the words of my mouth and the meditation of my heart be acceptable in Your sight, O Lord, my Rock and my Redeemer" (Psalm 19:14). Start with a clear intention to know God's will for your life and a fixed resolution in advance to do it.

- Slowly read the text again and again until it is in your short-term memory. Try making your first readings audible, since this will make them slower and more deliberate. (Bear in mind that in antiquity, reading always meant reading aloud.)

- Seek the meaning of the text; ask questions. But come more as a disciple than as a collector of information. See Scripture as iconographic; that is, a verbal window into the reality of life that turns your perspective around.

- Listen to the words in humility accompanied by a willingness to obey. Hearing the Word must be united by faith (Hebrews 4:2) with an intention to apply it in practice (James 1:22). Open yourself to be addressed by the Word in your attitudes, habits, choices, and emotions. There will be times when you resist a penetrating living encounter with God, and these generally have to do with areas of disobedience. Thus, it is wise to examine your being and doing in the light of the text by asking, *Lord, what are You saying to me in this passage?*

- Remember that unlike ordinary reading, in *lectio* you are seeking to be shaped by the Word more than informed by the Word. This first step of reading prepares you for the remaining three movements of meditation, prayer, and contemplation. But the whole process should be infused with a prayerful attitude.

- Avoid the usual pragmatic reflex that seeks to "net out" some immediate benefit. Approach sacred reading with no conditions, demands, or expectations. The Word may not meet your perceived needs, but it will touch your real needs, even when you don't discern them.

MEDITATION (MEDITATIO)

As you move from reading to meditation, you are seeking to saturate and immerse yourself in the Word, to luxuriate in its living waters, and to receive the words as an intimate and personal message from God. The purpose of meditation is to penetrate the Scriptures and to let them penetrate us through the loving gaze of the heart. The term *mental prayer* is often associated with meditation, but this could be misleading, because *lectio, meditatio,* and *oratio* involve not only the mind, but also the heart. Meditation attunes the inward self to the Holy Spirit so that our hearts harmonize and resonate with His voice. Meditation is a spiritual work of holy desire and an interior invitation for the Spirit to pray and speak within us (Romans 8:26-27) in such a way that our whole being is transformed into greater conformity with Jesus Christ. It is an intentional process of building our passion for Christ by meeting with Him and spending time with Him to know Him more clearly, to love Him more dearly, and to follow Him more nearly. By meditating on God's truth, we are inviting Christ to be formed in us (Galatians 4:19) by a deliberate dwelling on His words. Thus, mental prayer should not be seen as an abstract exercise but as a vital vehicle for the metamorphosis of the soul.

> *This book of the law shall not depart from your mouth, but you shall meditate on it day and night, so that you may be careful to do according to all that is written in it; for then you will make your way prosperous, and then you will have success.*
>
> —Joshua 1:8

This familiar verse tells us that the path to success *as God defines it* is the habit of making space in our lives to meet with God in His holy Word with a heartfelt intention to apply what He reveals through obedient action. Only those who delight in God's Word and habitually meditate on it (Psalm 1:2) will experience the fullness and stability of God's purpose and calling. May you be one of them.

Suggestions for Meditation

- Since it is God's love for us that teaches us to love Him, we should not regard meditation as an objective method or technique, but as a person-specific process. It is good to experiment with different approaches until you find a pattern of meditation that resonates best with your soul.
- Acknowledge the holiness of the God you are approaching and the richness of the gift of faith that makes it possible for you to enjoy an encounter with Him through His Spirit.
- Meditation is a long-term process that builds upon itself. The more we absorb Scripture, the greater our mental storehouse becomes. As this process continues for months and years, we experience the phenomenon of *reminiscence* in which a word or phrase spontaneously evokes a wealth of imagery from other parts of Scripture. This can be an exciting and creative experience in which we see connections and rhythms we never perceived before. These chain reactions, the fruit of habitual meditation, develop in us "the mind of Christ" (1 Corinthians 2:16).
- Allow enough time to enjoy the text; to rush this process is like running through a great art gallery.
- Meditation on Scripture involves ruminating (*ruminatio*) on a word, phrase, passage, or story. When we chew on the text in our minds, we

release the full flavor as we assimilate its content.

- Don't force meditation or make impatient demands of immediate gratification and results. Meditation will do you little good if you try to control the outcome.
- When you encounter something that speaks particularly to you, you should note it so that you can reflect on it later. You may find it helpful to make written reminders that you can carry with you.
- It may also be beneficial to keep a journal of your personal reflections on the text. If you do this, you will need to be open and honest with yourself in the things you record. The advantage of a journal is the creation of a private record that can be reviewed from time to time.
- Personalize the words of the text and "realize" them; receive them as God speaking to you in the present moment. Try to hear the passage as though for the first time, personally addressed to you.
- When a passage speaks to you, consider meditating on the same text for several days before moving on to another.
- The millions of images we have been exposed to through television, movies, magazines, newspapers, and other media have not sharpened but dulled our creative imagination. More than ever, we need to develop and sanctify our imagination, because the truth of Scripture and spiritual experience is, to use Jean Leclercq's words, "impregnated with a mysterious light impossible to analyze." A sanctified imagination will enable us to grasp more than we can see, but we need the lifeline of Scripture to tether us to the truth.
- Many people have found it helpful to engage the five senses when meditating on biblical stories, especially the stories in the Gospels. This process makes the scene more present and real to us and it helps us transition from the cognitive, analytical level to the affective, feeling level of our being.
- In addition to the imaginative use of the senses, it can be illuminating to put yourself in the story. How would you have reacted, and what would you have thought and said if you were there?
- The *Spiritual Exercises* of Ignatius of Loyola incorporates these and other meditative techniques and has useful insights on contemplating the incarnation, life, death, resurrection, and ascension of Christ. The various meditations and prayers prescribed in *Introduction to the Devout Life* by Francis de Sales (on such topics as our creation, the end for which we were created, sin, death, humility, and God's love for us) are also valuable resources for many. But because temperaments differ, not everyone will find such methodical meditation schemes helpful. Most people are sensory, but some are more analytical, and others are more intuitive. Intuitives will benefit more from savoring the truths of a passage than from its imagery. To quote Dom Chapman, "Pray as you can, not as you can't!"

- Meditation on the Psalms *(meditatio psalmorum)* has edified the saints for thousands of years and should be a regular part of our spiritual diet. It is enormously beneficial in all seasons and conditions of life to savor and absorb the meaning of the Psalms in the depths of one's heart.
- Ideally, meditation should address the mind, the emotions, and the will. Ruminating on Scripture stimulates our thinking and understanding and it also elevates the affections of the heart. It reaches the will when we resolve to let the passage shape our actions. Intellect, imagination, and volition should not be divorced from one another.
- Accept the fact that you will often encounter problems with distraction and inattention. Do not be disturbed when your mind wanders, but gently and calmly return to the text before you. As Thomas Merton stated in *New Seeds of Contemplation,* "It is much better to desire God without being able to think clearly of Him, than to have marvelous thoughts about Him without desiring to enter into union with His will." Normally, it is best to resist the temptation to be distracted by practical concerns, but sometimes it can be helpful to turn these concerns into subjects of meditation in light of the truth of the text.
- Remember that meditation does not need to produce evident affection or consolation in order to be beneficial. The quest for moving experiences can lead to the self-deception of emotional melodrama and counterfeit mysticism.

PRAYER (ORATIO)

The discipline of prayer is usually associated with a personal dialogue (colloquy) with God, though the majority of our prayers appear to be monologues in which we petition God. In *lectio divina,* prayer is specifically related to the two prior movements of sacred reading and meditation on the text. *Oratio* is the fruit of *meditatio,* and it is the way we "interiorize" what God has spoken to us through the passage. The transition from meditation to prayer may be subtle or unnoticed, but it is a response of the heart to what has been largely occupying the mind. It is a movement from truth to implication, from hearing to acknowledgment, from understanding to obedience.

Depending on how the living and active Word is shaping us (Hebrews 4:12), this period of prayer can be sweet and consoling, or it can be painful and revealing. The two-edged sword of the Spirit has a way of exposing the thoughts and intentions of the heart, and when our selfish, distorted, and manipulative strategies are "open and laid bare to the eyes of Him with whom we have to do" (Hebrews 4:13), *oratio* becomes a time for contrition, confession, and repentance. When the soul is exposed and we see our interior and exterior lives as God sees them, it can be both devastating (in light of God's holiness) and exhilarating (in light of God's forgiveness and compassion). At other times, we may be gripped by the power of spiritual truth (for example, the kindness and love of the Father, the grace and faithfulness of the Son, the fellowship and presence of the Spirit) and respond in adoration or thanksgiving. *Oratio* is a time for participation in the three interpenetrating Persons of the Trinity through prolonged mutual presence and growing identification with the life of Christ.

Suggestions for Prayer

- Allow enough time so that you do not rush the process; you are not likely to listen to God when you are in a hurry.
- Avoid the rut of reducing this period of prayer to a technique or a routine.
- In *lectio divina,* there is a temptation to substitute reading for prayer. It is helpful to view your reading and meditation on the text as preparation for a personal prayerful response.
- Do not seek to control the content or outcome of your prayer.
- Remember that *oratio* is a time for heart response as you move from the mind to the will. Prayer embraces the practical consequences of the truth you have seen and endeavors to direct your life in accordance with it.
- Depending on your reading and meditation, your response can take a number of different forms, including adoration, confession, renewal, petition, intercession, affirmation, and thanksgiving. All of these are different ways of calling upon the Lord, but at one time a prayer of adoration may be appropriate, while at another time the Spirit may lead you in a prayer of confession or petition.
- When the Lord speaks to you in the text by way of exhortation or encouragement, it is good to "pray it through" — that is, to take the time to internalize the message.
- See this time as an opportunity to move away from your false self (the flesh) toward your true self in Christ.
- Scripture is God-breathed and "profitable for teaching, for reproof, for correction, for training in righteousness" (2 Timothy 3:16). Invite the Spirit to search, teach, encourage, comfort, and correct you. Let Him reveal and dispel your illusions, pride, self-centeredness, stubbornness, ungodly attitudes and habits, stinginess, lack of gratitude, manipulation and control, and so forth.
- Prayer can occur at any time during the *lectio* process, and you may find yourself alternating between reading, meditation, and prayer. *Lectio divina* is not a lockstep, sequential movement.
- When you are distracted, simply return to the text to refocus your attention. Teresa of Avila used an image of prayer as a small fire that occasionally needs to be fed by adding a twig or two. A twig is a few words from Scripture, but too many words become branches that could extinguish the fire.
- Bear in mind that in *lectio divina,* prayer is part of the path that leads to contemplation.

CONTEMPLATION (CONTEMPLATIO)

Some who use the term *lectio divina* limit it primarily to slow, careful, and prayerful reading of a biblical passage, book, or other spiritual text rather than the whole movement from reading to meditation to prayer to contemplation. As I see it, however, the process of *lectio divina* should begin with reading and culminate in contemplation. Contemplation is often confused with meditation, but as we will see, they are not synonymous.

Meditation and the prayer that flows out of it bring us into communication with the living and transcendent Lord, and as such they prepare us for contemplation. Meditative prayer should be more than an intellectual exercise; when it is accompanied by affective intention it leads to the love and communion of contemplative prayer. Because of its very nature, it is notoriously difficult to communicate the characteristics of contemplative prayer. It is a mysterious territory in which the language is silence and the action is receptivity. True contemplation is a theological grace that cannot be reduced to logical, psychological, or aesthetic categories. Perhaps these general contrasts between meditative and contemplative prayer will help:

MEDITATIVE PRAYER	CONTEMPLATIVE PRAYER
Speech	Silence
Activity	Receptivity
Discursive thought	Loss of mental images and concepts
Vocal and mental prayer	Wordless prayer and interior stillness
Natural faculties of reason and imagination	Mysterious darkening of the natural faculties
Affective feelings	Loss of feelings
Reading and reflection	Inability to meditate
Doing	Being
Seeking	Receiving
Talking to Jesus	Entering into the prayer of Jesus

When he witnessed the miracle of the transfiguration of Jesus on the holy mountain, the awestruck Peter inappropriately broke into speech and was silenced by the voice out of the cloud that said, "This is My beloved Son, with whom I am well pleased; listen to Him!" (Matthew 17:4-5). When we enter into the numinous territory of contemplation, it is best for us to stop talking and "listen to Him" in simple and loving attentiveness. In this strange and holy land we must remove the sandals of our ideas, constructs, and inclinations, and quietly listen for the voice of God. Periods of contemplation can be little "dark nights of faith." During these times, God may seem absent and silent, but His presence and speech is on a deeper level than what we can feel or understand. By preparing a peaceful place in the soul we learn to "rest in the Lord and wait patiently for Him" (Psalm 37:7).

A number of people have been exposed to aspects of contemplative prayer through *centering prayer,* a practice that was recently revived and updated by three Cistercian monks—Thomas Keating, William Meninger, and Basil Pennington. This method of prayer is based on the fourteenth-century classic of mystical theology *The Cloud of Unknowing.* Another approach to contemplative prayer is the *prayer of the heart* that is described in the *Philokalia,* an anthology of quotations from Eastern monastic Fathers from the third century to the Middle Ages. In this tradition, the invocation of the name of the Lord Jesus is used to create a state of receptivity and interior recollection of the presence of God.

Suggestions for Contemplation

- Take enough time to present yourself before God in silence and yieldedness. Contemplative prayer involves the development of a deeper and more intuitive form of receptivity to the supernatural.
- As with meditation and prayer, do not be concerned with results, feelings, or experiences during contemplation. The important thing is to "appear before God" in a quiet and receptive mode of being.
- It is helpful to think of a word or an image that expresses what I call the *spirit of the passage* that you have been processing in your reading, meditation, and prayer. When your mind wanders during your time for contemplation, center yourself by returning once again to the spirit of the passage.
- Contemplation is a gift very few believers have attempted to develop. Expect that growth in this new terrain will involve time, discipline, and the frustration of apparent failure. Don't allow distractions or lack of initial benefits to dissuade you from this time-tested discipline. True contemplation may require years of fidelity, but any consistency in this practice will greatly reward you.
- Contemplation is especially difficult for more extroverted and sensory temperaments. This is a discipline of silence, of loss of control, of abandoning the attempt to analyze and intellectualize, and of developing the intuitive faculties.
- Remember that you cannot engage in contemplative prayer by your own effort; it is God's work, and it requires a *receptive passivity.* In contemplation it is best to abandon self-consciousness and to allow yourself to be drawn into the inexpressible depths of God's love.
- Because *lectio divina* is not a rigid movement through four steps, you may find yourself going back to reading, meditation, or prayer and returning again to the interior silence of contemplation. The amount of time you spend in each of these four elements is up to you, and you should experiment with this. However, I recommend that you practice

all four since each of them has a unique benefit.
- Nourish your interior life by reducing your exposure to radio, television, and other forms of distraction and commotion.

My colleague George Grove uses the following set of analogies to integrate the four components of sacred reading:

LECTIO	MEDITATIO	ORATIO	CONTEMPLATIO
Read	Meditate	Pray	Abide
Lips	Mind	Heart	Spirit
Seek	Find	Knock	Open
Food	Chew	Savor	Fill

Lectio divina engages the whole person from the physical to the psychological to the inward spiritual center of our being. It promotes a harmonious unity through an organic process that uses a variety of means. Fidelity and consistency in this long-term activity will gradually enhance and enrich your life.

Suggestions for Sacred Reading As a Whole

- Do not reduce sacred reading to a technique, system, or program. It has been called a *methodless method* that contributes to the development of a mode of being toward God. It is a personal process that cultivates a spiritual outlook of trust, receptivity, expectation, worship, and intimacy with God.
- Always see yourself as a beginner in the sense that you never "master" this process. There is always more than we think. Remember that discipline and devotion reinforce each other.
- Feel free to adapt this spiritual formation approach to your temperament. More extroverted people, for example, will only be comfortable with short sessions, while more introverted people will tend to take more time in this process.
- Perhaps the most important suggestion I can make is for you to write out the verse or verses you have used for sacred reading on a given day and carry this card with you through your activities. By doing this, you are making that day's passage your theme for twenty-four hours and using it as a tool to practice the presence of Christ. These cards can also assist you in memorization by moving the texts from short-term to longer-term memory.
- It is possible for some personality types to develop a false supernaturalism by becoming immersed in an artificial experience. Thinking they are communing with God, they are really lost in themselves. This problem of self-delusion and misguided zeal can be corrected by a willingness

to accept sound advice through spiritual direction.

- To aspire to contemplation without cultivating compassion for others is to miss the point and purpose of contemplative prayer. The byproduct of devotional spirituality should always be an increased capacity to love and serve others. By the same token, a growing realization of our union with others in Christ will enhance our capacity to know God.

A BLEND OF CONTEMPLATION AND ACTION

The polarity between the contemplative life and the active life has been a source of tension for many centuries. Saint Gregory advocated a more contemplative approach to prayer as rest from exterior action in the quest for communion with God. Saint Basil promoted a more active approach to prayer in association with work. Carried too far, the contemplative extreme could divorce our primary calling to know God from our secondary calling to express this knowledge in the world. On the other hand, the active extreme tends to elevate our secondary calling of work to the point of replacing our primary calling. A more balanced approach integrates and honors both callings and unites the contemplative and active vocations. Saint Benedict encouraged this blended rhythm of rest and action, interior aspiration and exterior obedience, devotion and discipline, prayer and labor, desire for God and service of neighbor, the spring of living water and the stream that flows out of it. By uniting the strengths of both Mary and Martha, we can learn to be contemplatives in action.

CULTIVATING A PASSION FOR CHRIST

Devotional spirituality is like a delicate grapevine that flourishes only when it is planted in the right soil and carefully cultivated in a good climate. Unless it is nurtured, it will wither from neglect and fail to bear fruit. The fruit of spiritual passion can be threatened by natural enemies, but it can also be stimulated by several sources.

Enemies of Spiritual Passion

- *Unresolved areas of disobedience.* Resisting the prodding of God in an area of your life may seem subtle, but it can be a more serious grievance to the heart of God than we suppose. It is good to invite the Holy Spirit to reveal any barriers in our relationship with God or people that have been erected by sinful attitudes and actions. When these become evident, deal with them quickly and trust in the power of God's forgiveness through the blood of Christ.
- *Complacency.* Without holy desire we will succumb to the sin of spiritual *acedia:* indifference, apathy, and boredom. People who lose the sharp edge of intention and calling can slip into a morass of listlessness and feelings of failure. We must often ask God for the grace of acute desire

so that we will hunger and thirst for Him.

- *Erosion in spiritual disciplines.* Complacency can cause or be caused by a failure to train and remain disciplined in the spiritual life. There are several biblical figures like King Asa (2 Chronicles 14–16) who illustrate the problem of starting well in the first half of life and finishing poorly in the last half. When spiritual disciplines begin to erode, spiritual passion declines as well.
- *External obedience.* There are many people who are more concerned about conformity to rules, moral behavior, and duty than they are about loving Jesus. External obedience without inward affection falls short of the biblical vision of obeying God from the heart (Jeremiah 31:33; Romans 6:17; Ephesians 6:6).
- *Loving truth more than Christ.* Some students of the Word have come to love the content of truth in the Bible more than the Source of that truth. Biblical and systematic theology are worthy of pursuit, but not when they become substitutes for the pursuit of knowing and becoming like Jesus.
- *Elevating service and ministry above Christ.* It is easier to define ourselves by what we accomplish than by our new identity in Christ. For some, the Christian life consists more of fellowship, service to those in need, witnessing, and worship than of becoming intimate with Jesus. This leads to the problem of ministry without the manifest presence of God.
- *Greater commitment to institutions than to Christ.* It is easy for churches, denominations, or other organizations to occupy more of our time and attention than devotion to Jesus. There is a constant danger of getting more passionate about causes than about Christ.
- *A merely functional relationship.* Many people are more interested in what Jesus can do for them than in who He is. We may initially come to Him hoping that He will help us with our career, marriage, children, or health, but if we do not grow beyond this "gifts above the Giver" mentality, we will never develop spiritual passion.

Sources of Spiritual Passion

- *Growing awareness of God as a Person.* God is an intensely personal and relational Being, and it is an insult for us to treat Him as though He were a power or a principle. Some of us find it easier to be comfortable with abstract principles and ideas than with people and intimacy. As we have seen, good things like the Bible, theology, ministry, and church can become substitutes for loving Him. As a countermeasure, it is good to ask God for the grace of increased passion for His Son so that, by the power of the Spirit, we will come to love Him as the Father loves Him.
- *Sitting at Jesus' feet.* When we make consistent time for reading, meditation, prayer, and contemplation, we place ourselves at the feet of Jesus and enjoy His presence. By making ourselves available and receptive to

Him, we learn the wisdom of spending more time being a friend of Jesus than a friend of others.

- *Imitating the Master.* Our identification with Jesus in His death, burial, resurrection, and ascension has made us new creatures before God (2 Corinthians 5:17). This divinely wrought identification makes it possible for us to imitate Jesus and "follow in His steps" (1 Peter 2:21). If we love the Master, we will want to be like Him in His character, humility, compassion, love, joy, peace, and dependence on the Father's will.

- *Cultivating spiritual affections.* Regardless of our natural temperaments, it is important for us to develop true affections (desire, longing, zeal, craving, hunger) for God. The rich emotional life of the psalmists (see Psalm 27:4; 42:1-3; 63:1-8; 145:1-21) reveals a desire for God above all else and a willingness to cling to Him during times of aridity and dryness. Like them, we must aspire to a love that is beyond us (Ephesians 3:17-19).

- *Increasing appreciation for the goodness of God.* The distractions of the world make it difficult for us to develop a growing appreciation for our relationship with God. We forget that we can enjoy communion with Someone who is infinitely better than the objects of our most powerful natural desires. We must pray for the grace of gratitude and amazement at the unqualified goodness of God's "kindness toward us in Christ Jesus" (Ephesians 2:7).

- *Focused intention.* What do you want (or want to want) more than anything else? God is pleased when we pursue Him with a heart that is intent on knowing and loving Him. He "begins His influence by working in us that we may have the will, and He completes it by working with us when we have the will" (Augustine, *On Grace and Free Will*). As our wills become more simplified and centered on becoming like Jesus, our love for Him will grow.

- *Willingness to let God break the outward self.* "Unless a grain of wheat falls into the earth and dies, it remains alone; but if it dies, it bears much fruit. He who loves his life loses it, and he who hates his life in this world will keep it to life eternal" (John 12:24-25). The alabaster vial of the self-life must be broken (Mark 14:3) to release the perfume of the new self in Christ. If we wish to manifest the fragrance of Christ, we must allow God to bring us (in His time and way) to the painful place of brokenness on the cross of self-abandonment to Him. This theme resonates in spiritual literature, and one of the clearest expressions is in Watchman Nee's *The Release of the Spirit*.

- *Desiring to please God more than to impress people.* If we want to be like Christ, we must embrace His governing goal to be pleasing to the Father (John 8:29; Hebrews 10:7). The enemy of this glorious goal is the competing quest for human approval (John 5:41,44; 12:43; Galatians 1:10). We cannot have it both ways; we will either play to an Audience of One or to an audience of many. But in the end, only God's opinion will matter.

- *Treasuring God.* Dallas Willard observes in *The Divine Conspiracy* that God "treasures those whom he has created, planned for, longed for, sorrowed over, redeemed, and befriended." Just as God has treasured us, so He wants us to respond by treasuring Him above all else. "We love, because He first loved us" (1 John 4:19)—the more we realize how God loved and valued us, the greater our capacity to love and value Him. In *Beginning to Pray,* Anthony Bloom suggests that one way to treasure God is to find a personal name or expression for God that flows out of our relationship with Him, like David's "You, my Joy!"
- *Maturing in trust.* As believers, we trust Christ for our eternal destiny, but most of us find it difficult to trust Him in our daily practice. As long as we pursue sinful strategies of seeking satisfaction on our own terms, our confidence will be misplaced. We must learn to trust Jesus enough to place our confidence in His power, not in our performance.

GETTING THE MOST OUT OF THIS JOURNAL

This is one of four journals in the *Reflections* series, and it is designed to guide you through three months of sacred reading passages. I have selected ninety texts from the Psalms that are particularly well suited to the process of sacred reading. These texts range from one to several verses, and they are arranged in biblical sequence. I have translated the verses from the original languages, and in several cases I have adapted and personalized these passages.

The daily four-part sequence of reading, meditation, prayer, and contemplation invites you to engage personally with the text and to record your thoughts and prayers in the process. This journaling component will enhance your interaction with each of the readings, and it will yield a valuable record of your reflections and prayers during these months. When you have completed this journal of sacred readings, you will profit from reading through the comments and prayers you have recorded.

I also suggest you go through this process a second time and visit each of these passages once again. You will discover new things in the Scripture texts that you did not see the first time through.

> *May the God of our Lord Jesus Christ, the Father of glory, give you a spirit of wisdom and of revelation in the full knowledge of Him, and may the eyes of your heart be enlightened, in order that you may know what is the hope of His calling, what are the riches of His glorious inheritance in the saints, and what is the incomparable greatness of His power toward us who believe.*
>
> —Ephesians 1:17-19

O my soul, above all things and in all things always rest in the Lord, for He is the eternal rest of the saints.

Grant me most sweet and loving Jesus, to rest in You above every other creature, above all health and beauty, above all glory and honor, above all power and dignity, above all knowledge and precise thought, above all wealth and talent, above all joy and exultation, above all fame and praise, above all sweetness and consolation, above all hope and promise, above all merit and desire, above all gifts and favors You give and shower upon me, above all happiness and joy that the mind can understand and feel, and finally, above all angels and archangels, above all the hosts of heaven, above all things visible and invisible, and above all that is not You, my God.

—Thomas à Kempis, *The Imitation of Christ*

SCRIPTURE

When I consider Your heavens, the work of Your fingers,
The moon and the stars, which You have set in place,
What is man that You are mindful of him,
And the son of man that You care for him?
You made him a little lower than the heavenly beings
And crowned him with glory and honor.
You made him ruler over the works of Your hands,
And You put everything under his feet. (Psalm 8:3-6)

READING

Slowly read the Scripture passage several times.

MEDITATION

Take some time to reflect on the words and phrases in the text.
Which words, phrases, or images speak most to you?

PRAYER

Offer the internalized passage back to God in the form of a personalized
prayer of adoration, confession, renewal, petition, intercession,
affirmation, or thanksgiving.

CONTEMPLATION

What word or image captures the spirit of the passage for you?

Take a few minutes to present yourself before God in silence and
yieldedness. When your mind wanders, center yourself by returning
to the spirit of the passage.

SCRIPTURE

I will praise You, O Lord, with all my heart;
I will tell of all Your wonders.
I will be glad and rejoice in You;
I will sing praise to Your name, O Most High. (Psalm 9:1-2)

READING

Slowly read the Scripture passage several times.

MEDITATION

Take some time to reflect on the words and phrases in the text.
Which words, phrases, or images speak most to you?

PRAYER

Offer the internalized passage back to God in the form of a personalized
prayer of adoration, confession, renewal, petition, intercession,
affirmation, or thanksgiving.

CONTEMPLATION

What word or image captures the spirit of the passage for you?

Take a few minutes to present yourself before God in silence and
yieldedness. When your mind wanders, center yourself by returning
to the spirit of the passage.

SCRIPTURE

The Lord reigns forever;
He has established His throne for judgment.
He will judge the world in righteousness,
And He will govern the peoples with justice.
The Lord will also be a refuge for the oppressed,
A stronghold in times of trouble.
Those who know Your name will trust in You,
For You, Lord, have never forsaken those who seek You. (Psalm 9:7-10)

READING

Slowly read the Scripture passage several times.

MEDITATION

Take some time to reflect on the words and phrases in the text.
Which words, phrases, or images speak most to you?

PRAYER

Offer the internalized passage back to God in the form of a personalized
prayer of adoration, confession, renewal, petition, intercession,
affirmation, or thanksgiving.

CONTEMPLATION

What word or image captures the spirit of the passage for you?

Take a few minutes to present yourself before God in silence and
yieldedness. When your mind wanders, center yourself by returning
to the spirit of the passage.

SCRIPTURE

Lord, who may dwell in Your tabernacle?
Who may live on Your holy mountain?
He who walks uprightly and works righteousness
And speaks the truth in his heart;
He does not slander with his tongue
Nor does evil to his neighbor
Nor takes up a reproach against his friend;
He despises the reprobate
But honors those who fear the Lord.
He keeps his oath even when it hurts,
Lends his money without interest,
And does not accept a bribe against the innocent.
He who does these things will never be shaken. (Psalm 15)

READING

Slowly read the Scripture passage several times.

MEDITATION

Take some time to reflect on the words and phrases in the text.
Which words, phrases, or images speak most to you?

PRAYER

Offer the internalized passage back to God in the form of a personalized
prayer of adoration, confession, renewal, petition, intercession,
affirmation, or thanksgiving.

CONTEMPLATION

What word or image captures the spirit of the passage for you?

Take a few minutes to present yourself before God in silence and
yieldedness. When your mind wanders, center yourself by returning
to the spirit of the passage.

SCRIPTURE

I have set the Lord always before me;
Because He is at my right hand, I will not be shaken.
Therefore my heart is glad, and my glory rejoices;
My body also will rest in hope.
You will make known to me the path of life;
In Your presence is fullness of joy;
In Your right hand are pleasures forever. (Psalm 16:8-9,11)

READING

Slowly read the Scripture passage several times.

MEDITATION

Take some time to reflect on the words and phrases in the text.
Which words, phrases, or images speak most to you?

PRAYER

Offer the internalized passage back to God in the form of a personalized
prayer of adoration, confession, renewal, petition, intercession,
affirmation, or thanksgiving.

CONTEMPLATION

What word or image captures the spirit of the passage for you?

Take a few minutes to present yourself before God in silence and
yieldedness. When your mind wanders, center yourself by returning
to the spirit of the passage.

READING 6

SCRIPTURE

As for God, His way is perfect;
The word of the Lord is proven.
He is a shield to all who take refuge in Him.
For who is God besides the Lord?
And who is the Rock except our God? (Psalm 18:30-31)

READING

Slowly read the Scripture passage several times.

MEDITATION

Take some time to reflect on the words and phrases in the text.
Which words, phrases, or images speak most to you?

PRAYER

Offer the internalized passage back to God in the form of a personalized
prayer of adoration, confession, renewal, petition, intercession,
affirmation, or thanksgiving.

CONTEMPLATION

What word or image captures the spirit of the passage for you?

Take a few minutes to present yourself before God in silence and
yieldedness. When your mind wanders, center yourself by returning
to the spirit of the passage.

SCRIPTURE

The heavens declare the glory of God,
And the skies proclaim the work of His hands.
Day after day they pour forth speech;
Night after night they reveal knowledge. (Psalm 19:1-2)

READING

Slowly read the Scripture passage several times.

MEDITATION

Take some time to reflect on the words and phrases in the text.
Which words, phrases, or images speak most to you?

PRAYER

Offer the internalized passage back to God in the form of a personalized
prayer of adoration, confession, renewal, petition, intercession,
affirmation, or thanksgiving.

CONTEMPLATION

What word or image captures the spirit of the passage for you?

Take a few minutes to present yourself before God in silence and
yieldedness. When your mind wanders, center yourself by returning
to the spirit of the passage.

SCRIPTURE

Let the words of my mouth and the meditation of my heart
Be pleasing in Your sight,
O Lord, my Rock and my Redeemer. (Psalm 19:14)

READING

Slowly read the Scripture passage several times.

MEDITATION

Take some time to reflect on the words and phrases in the text.
Which words, phrases, or images speak most to you?

PRAYER

Offer the internalized passage back to God in the form of a personalized
prayer of adoration, confession, renewal, petition, intercession,
affirmation, or thanksgiving.

CONTEMPLATION

What word or image captures the spirit of the passage for you?

Take a few minutes to present yourself before God in silence and
yieldedness. When your mind wanders, center yourself by returning
to the spirit of the passage.

SCRIPTURE

The Lord is my shepherd;
I shall not be in want.
He makes me lie down in green pastures;
He leads me beside quiet waters;
He restores my soul.
He guides me in the paths of righteousness
For His name's sake.
Even though I walk through the valley of the shadow of death,
I will fear no evil, for You are with me;
Your rod and Your staff, they comfort me.
You prepare a table before me in the presence of my enemies.
You anoint my head with oil;
My cup overflows.
Surely goodness and mercy will follow me all the days of my life,
And I will dwell in the house of the Lord forever. (Psalm 23)

READING

Slowly read the Scripture passage several times.

MEDITATION

Take some time to reflect on the words and phrases in the text.
Which words, phrases, or images speak most to you?

PRAYER

Offer the internalized passage back to God in the form of a personalized
prayer of adoration, confession, renewal, petition, intercession,
affirmation, or thanksgiving.

CONTEMPLATION

What word or image captures the spirit of the passage for you?

Take a few minutes to present yourself before God in silence and
yieldedness. When your mind wanders, center yourself by returning
to the spirit of the passage.

SCRIPTURE

The earth is the Lord's, and everything in it,
The world and all who dwell in it.
For He founded it upon the seas
And established it upon the waters. (Psalm 24:1-2)

READING

Slowly read the Scripture passage several times.

MEDITATION

Take some time to reflect on the words and phrases in the text.
Which words, phrases, or images speak most to you?

PRAYER

Offer the internalized passage back to God in the form of a personalized
prayer of adoration, confession, renewal, petition, intercession,
affirmation, or thanksgiving.

CONTEMPLATION

What word or image captures the spirit of the passage for you?

Take a few minutes to present yourself before God in silence and
yieldedness. When your mind wanders, center yourself by returning
to the spirit of the passage.

SCRIPTURE

Who may ascend the hill of the Lord?
Who may stand in His holy place?
He who has clean hands and a pure heart,
Who has not lifted up his soul to an idol
Or sworn by what is false. (Psalm 24:3-4)

READING

Slowly read the Scripture passage several times.

MEDITATION

Take some time to reflect on the words and phrases in the text.
Which words, phrases, or images speak most to you?

PRAYER

Offer the internalized passage back to God in the form of a personalized
prayer of adoration, confession, renewal, petition, intercession,
affirmation, or thanksgiving.

CONTEMPLATION

What word or image captures the spirit of the passage for you?

Take a few minutes to present yourself before God in silence and
yieldedness. When your mind wanders, center yourself by returning
to the spirit of the passage.

SCRIPTURE

No one who waits for You will be ashamed,
But those who are treacherous without cause will be ashamed.
Show me Your ways, O Lord,
Teach me Your paths;
Lead me in Your truth and teach me,
For You are the God of my salvation,
And my hope is in You all day long. (Psalm 25:3-5)

READING

Slowly read the Scripture passage several times.

MEDITATION

Take some time to reflect on the words and phrases in the text.
Which words, phrases, or images speak most to you?

PRAYER

Offer the internalized passage back to God in the form of a personalized prayer of adoration, confession, renewal, petition, intercession, affirmation, or thanksgiving.

CONTEMPLATION

What word or image captures the spirit of the passage for you?

Take a few minutes to present yourself before God in silence and yieldedness. When your mind wanders, center yourself by returning to the spirit of the passage.

SCRIPTURE

I would have lost heart
Unless I had believed that I would see the goodness of the Lord
In the land of the living.
I will hope in the Lord
And be of good courage, and He will strengthen my heart;
Yes, I will hope in the Lord. (Psalm 27:13-14)

READING

Slowly read the Scripture passage several times.

MEDITATION

Take some time to reflect on the words and phrases in the text.
Which words, phrases, or images speak most to you?

PRAYER

Offer the internalized passage back to God in the form of a personalized
prayer of adoration, confession, renewal, petition, intercession,
affirmation, or thanksgiving.

CONTEMPLATION

What word or image captures the spirit of the passage for you?

Take a few minutes to present yourself before God in silence and
yieldedness. When your mind wanders, center yourself by returning
to the spirit of the passage.

SCRIPTURE

The Lord is my strength and my shield;
My heart trusts in Him, and I am helped.
My heart greatly rejoices,
And I will give thanks to Him in song. (Psalm 28:7)

READING

Slowly read the Scripture passage several times.

MEDITATION

Take some time to reflect on the words and phrases in the text.
Which words, phrases, or images speak most to you?

PRAYER

Offer the internalized passage back to God in the form of a personalized
prayer of adoration, confession, renewal, petition, intercession,
affirmation, or thanksgiving.

CONTEMPLATION

What word or image captures the spirit of the passage for you?

Take a few minutes to present yourself before God in silence and
yieldedness. When your mind wanders, center yourself by returning
to the spirit of the passage.

SCRIPTURE

I will ascribe to the Lord glory and strength.
I will ascribe to the Lord the glory due His name
And worship the Lord in the beauty of holiness. (Psalm 29:1-2)

READING

Slowly read the Scripture passage several times.

MEDITATION

Take some time to reflect on the words and phrases in the text.
Which words, phrases, or images speak most to you?

PRAYER

Offer the internalized passage back to God in the form of a personalized
prayer of adoration, confession, renewal, petition, intercession,
affirmation, or thanksgiving.

CONTEMPLATION

What word or image captures the spirit of the passage for you?

Take a few minutes to present yourself before God in silence and
yieldedness. When your mind wanders, center yourself by returning
to the spirit of the passage.

SCRIPTURE

I will sing praises to the Lord
And give thanks at the remembrance of His holy name.
For His anger lasts only a moment,
But His favor is for a lifetime;
Weeping may endure for a night,
But joy comes in the morning. (Psalm 30:4-5)

READING

Slowly read the Scripture passage several times.

MEDITATION

Take some time to reflect on the words and phrases in the text.
Which words, phrases, or images speak most to you?

PRAYER

Offer the internalized passage back to God in the form of a personalized
prayer of adoration, confession, renewal, petition, intercession,
affirmation, or thanksgiving.

CONTEMPLATION

What word or image captures the spirit of the passage for you?

Take a few minutes to present yourself before God in silence and
yieldedness. When your mind wanders, center yourself by returning
to the spirit of the passage.

SCRIPTURE

In You, O Lord, I have taken refuge;
Let me never be ashamed;
Deliver me in Your righteousness.
Since You are my rock and my fortress,
For Your name's sake lead me and guide me.
Into Your hands I commit my spirit;
Redeem me, O Lord, God of truth. (Psalm 31:1,3,5)

READING

Slowly read the Scripture passage several times.

MEDITATION

Take some time to reflect on the words and phrases in the text.
Which words, phrases, or images speak most to you?

PRAYER

Offer the internalized passage back to God in the form of a personalized
prayer of adoration, confession, renewal, petition, intercession,
affirmation, or thanksgiving.

CONTEMPLATION

What word or image captures the spirit of the passage for you?

Take a few minutes to present yourself before God in silence and
yieldedness. When your mind wanders, center yourself by returning
to the spirit of the passage.

SCRIPTURE

The word of the Lord is upright,
And all His work is done in faithfulness.
He loves righteousness and justice;
The earth is full of the lovingkindness of the Lord. (Psalm 33:4-5)

READING

Slowly read the Scripture passage several times.

MEDITATION

Take some time to reflect on the words and phrases in the text.
Which words, phrases, or images speak most to you?

PRAYER

Offer the internalized passage back to God in the form of a personalized prayer of adoration, confession, renewal, petition, intercession, affirmation, or thanksgiving.

CONTEMPLATION

What word or image captures the spirit of the passage for you?

Take a few minutes to present yourself before God in silence and yieldedness. When your mind wanders, center yourself by returning to the spirit of the passage.

SCRIPTURE

The counsel of the Lord stands firm forever,
The plans of His heart through all generations. (Psalm 33:11)

READING

Slowly read the Scripture passage several times.

MEDITATION

Take some time to reflect on the words and phrases in the text.
Which words, phrases, or images speak most to you?

PRAYER

Offer the internalized passage back to God in the form of a personalized
prayer of adoration, confession, renewal, petition, intercession,
affirmation, or thanksgiving.

CONTEMPLATION

What word or image captures the spirit of the passage for you?

Take a few minutes to present yourself before God in silence and
yieldedness. When your mind wanders, center yourself by returning
to the spirit of the passage.

SCRIPTURE

Come, my children, listen to me;
I will teach you the fear of the Lord.
Who is the man who desires life
And loves many days that he may see good?
Keep your tongue from evil
And your lips from speaking guile.
Depart from evil and do good;
Seek peace and pursue it.
The eyes of the Lord are on the righteous,
And His ears are attentive to their cry. (Psalm 34:11-15)

READING

Slowly read the Scripture passage several times.

MEDITATION

Take some time to reflect on the words and phrases in the text.
Which words, phrases, or images speak most to you?

PRAYER

Offer the internalized passage back to God in the form of a personalized prayer of adoration, confession, renewal, petition, intercession, affirmation, or thanksgiving.

CONTEMPLATION

What word or image captures the spirit of the passage for you?

Take a few minutes to present yourself before God in silence and yieldedness. When your mind wanders, center yourself by returning to the spirit of the passage.

SCRIPTURE

Your lovingkindness, O Lord, reaches to the heavens,
Your faithfulness to the skies.
Your righteousness is like the mountains of God;
Your judgments are like a great deep.
O Lord, You preserve man and beast.
How priceless is Your lovingkindness, O God!
The children of men find refuge in the shadow of Your wings.
For with You is the fountain of life;
In Your light we see light. (Psalm 36:5-7,9)

READING

Slowly read the Scripture passage several times.

MEDITATION

Take some time to reflect on the words and phrases in the text.
Which words, phrases, or images speak most to you?

PRAYER

Offer the internalized passage back to God in the form of a personalized prayer of adoration, confession, renewal, petition, intercession, affirmation, or thanksgiving.

CONTEMPLATION

What word or image captures the spirit of the passage for you?

Take a few minutes to present yourself before God in silence and yieldedness. When your mind wanders, center yourself by returning to the spirit of the passage.

SCRIPTURE

The salvation of the righteous comes from the Lord;
He is their stronghold in time of trouble.
The Lord helps them and delivers them;
He delivers them from the wicked and saves them,
Because they take refuge in Him. (Psalm 37:39-40)

READING

Slowly read the Scripture passage several times.

MEDITATION

Take some time to reflect on the words and phrases in the text.
Which words, phrases, or images speak most to you?

PRAYER

Offer the internalized passage back to God in the form of a personalized
prayer of adoration, confession, renewal, petition, intercession,
affirmation, or thanksgiving.

CONTEMPLATION

What word or image captures the spirit of the passage for you?

Take a few minutes to present yourself before God in silence and
yieldedness. When your mind wanders, center yourself by returning
to the spirit of the passage.

SCRIPTURE

God lifted me out of the slimy pit, out of the mud and mire;
He set my feet on a rock and gave me a firm place to stand.
He put a new song in my mouth, a hymn of praise to our God.
Many will see and fear and put their trust in the Lord. (Psalm 40:2-3)

READING

Slowly read the Scripture passage several times.

MEDITATION

Take some time to reflect on the words and phrases in the text.
Which words, phrases, or images speak most to you?

PRAYER

Offer the internalized passage back to God in the form of a personalized
prayer of adoration, confession, renewal, petition, intercession,
affirmation, or thanksgiving.

CONTEMPLATION

What word or image captures the spirit of the passage for you?

Take a few minutes to present yourself before God in silence and
yieldedness. When your mind wanders, center yourself by returning
to the spirit of the passage.

SCRIPTURE

Many, O Lord my God, are the wonders You have done,
And Your thoughts toward us no one can recount to You;
Were I to speak and tell of them,
They would be too many to declare. (Psalm 40:5)

READING

Slowly read the Scripture passage several times.

MEDITATION

Take some time to reflect on the words and phrases in the text.
Which words, phrases, or images speak most to you?

PRAYER

Offer the internalized passage back to God in the form of a personalized
prayer of adoration, confession, renewal, petition, intercession,
affirmation, or thanksgiving.

CONTEMPLATION

What word or image captures the spirit of the passage for you?

Take a few minutes to present yourself before God in silence and
yieldedness. When your mind wanders, center yourself by returning
to the spirit of the passage.

SCRIPTURE

Blessed be the Lord, the God of Israel,
From everlasting to everlasting.
Amen and Amen. (Psalm 41:13)

READING

Slowly read the Scripture passage several times.

MEDITATION

Take some time to reflect on the words and phrases in the text.
Which words, phrases, or images speak most to you?

PRAYER

Offer the internalized passage back to God in the form of a personalized
prayer of adoration, confession, renewal, petition, intercession,
affirmation, or thanksgiving.

CONTEMPLATION

What word or image captures the spirit of the passage for you?

Take a few minutes to present yourself before God in silence and
yieldedness. When your mind wanders, center yourself by returning
to the spirit of the passage.

SCRIPTURE

Why are you downcast, O my soul?
Why are you disturbed within me?
Hope in God, for I will yet praise Him
For the help of His presence.
O my God, my soul is downcast within me;
Therefore I will remember You.
Why are you downcast, O my soul?
Why are you disturbed within me?
Hope in God, for I will yet praise Him,
The help of my countenance and my God. (Psalm 42:5-6,11)

READING

Slowly read the Scripture passage several times.

MEDITATION

Take some time to reflect on the words and phrases in the text.
Which words, phrases, or images speak most to you?

PRAYER

Offer the internalized passage back to God in the form of a personalized
prayer of adoration, confession, renewal, petition, intercession,
affirmation, or thanksgiving.

CONTEMPLATION

What word or image captures the spirit of the passage for you?

Take a few minutes to present yourself before God in silence and
yieldedness. When your mind wanders, center yourself by returning
to the spirit of the passage.

SCRIPTURE

God is my refuge and strength,
An ever-present help in trouble.
Therefore I will not fear, though the earth changes
And the mountains slip into the heart of the sea. (Psalm 46:1-2)

READING

Slowly read the Scripture passage several times.

MEDITATION

Take some time to reflect on the words and phrases in the text.
Which words, phrases, or images speak most to you?

PRAYER

Offer the internalized passage back to God in the form of a personalized
prayer of adoration, confession, renewal, petition, intercession,
affirmation, or thanksgiving.

CONTEMPLATION

What word or image captures the spirit of the passage for you?

Take a few minutes to present yourself before God in silence and
yieldedness. When your mind wanders, center yourself by returning
to the spirit of the passage.

SCRIPTURE

I will be still and know that You are God;
You will be exalted among the nations,
You will be exalted in the earth. (Psalm 46:10)

READING

Slowly read the Scripture passage several times.

MEDITATION

Take some time to reflect on the words and phrases in the text.
Which words, phrases, or images speak most to you?

PRAYER

Offer the internalized passage back to God in the form of a personalized
prayer of adoration, confession, renewal, petition, intercession,
affirmation, or thanksgiving.

CONTEMPLATION

What word or image captures the spirit of the passage for you?

Take a few minutes to present yourself before God in silence and
yieldedness. When your mind wanders, center yourself by returning
to the spirit of the passage.

SCRIPTURE

The Lord Most High is awesome,
The great King over all the earth!
God is the King of all the earth,
And I will sing His praise.
God reigns over the nations;
God is seated on His holy throne. (Psalm 47:2,7-8)

READING

Slowly read the Scripture passage several times.

MEDITATION

Take some time to reflect on the words and phrases in the text.
Which words, phrases, or images speak most to you?

PRAYER

Offer the internalized passage back to God in the form of a personalized
prayer of adoration, confession, renewal, petition, intercession,
affirmation, or thanksgiving.

CONTEMPLATION

What word or image captures the spirit of the passage for you?

Take a few minutes to present yourself before God in silence and
yieldedness. When your mind wanders, center yourself by returning
to the spirit of the passage.

SCRIPTURE

Great is the Lord, and most worthy of praise
In the city of our God, His holy mountain.
As is Your name, O God,
So is Your praise to the ends of the earth;
Your right hand is filled with righteousness. (Psalm 48:1,10)

READING

Slowly read the Scripture passage several times.

MEDITATION

Take some time to reflect on the words and phrases in the text. Which words, phrases, or images speak most to you?

PRAYER

Offer the internalized passage back to God in the form of a personalized prayer of adoration, confession, renewal, petition, intercession, affirmation, or thanksgiving.

CONTEMPLATION

What word or image captures the spirit of the passage for you?

Take a few minutes to present yourself before God in silence and yieldedness. When your mind wanders, center yourself by returning to the spirit of the passage.

SCRIPTURE

The sacrifices of God are a broken spirit;
A broken and contrite heart, O God, You will not despise. (Psalm 51:17)

READING

Slowly read the Scripture passage several times.

MEDITATION

Take some time to reflect on the words and phrases in the text.
Which words, phrases, or images speak most to you?

PRAYER

Offer the internalized passage back to God in the form of a personalized
prayer of adoration, confession, renewal, petition, intercession,
affirmation, or thanksgiving.

CONTEMPLATION

What word or image captures the spirit of the passage for you?

Take a few minutes to present yourself before God in silence and
yieldedness. When your mind wanders, center yourself by returning
to the spirit of the passage.

SCRIPTURE

I will praise You forever for what You have done;
I will hope in Your name, for it is good.
I will praise You in the presence of Your saints. (Psalm 52:9)

READING

Slowly read the Scripture passage several times.

MEDITATION

Take some time to reflect on the words and phrases in the text.
Which words, phrases, or images speak most to you?

PRAYER

Offer the internalized passage back to God in the form of a personalized prayer of adoration, confession, renewal, petition, intercession, affirmation, or thanksgiving.

CONTEMPLATION

What word or image captures the spirit of the passage for you?

Take a few minutes to present yourself before God in silence and yieldedness. When your mind wanders, center yourself by returning to the spirit of the passage.

SCRIPTURE

When I am afraid, I will trust in You.
In God, whose word I praise,
In God I have put my trust.
I will not fear;
What can mortal man do to me? (Psalm 56:3-4)

READING

Slowly read the Scripture passage several times.

MEDITATION

Take some time to reflect on the words and phrases in the text.
Which words, phrases, or images speak most to you?

PRAYER

Offer the internalized passage back to God in the form of a personalized
prayer of adoration, confession, renewal, petition, intercession,
affirmation, or thanksgiving.

CONTEMPLATION

What word or image captures the spirit of the passage for you?

Take a few minutes to present yourself before God in silence and
yieldedness. When your mind wanders, center yourself by returning
to the spirit of the passage.

SCRIPTURE

Have mercy on me, O God, have mercy on me,
For in You my soul takes refuge.
I will take refuge in the shadow of Your wings
Until destruction passes by.
I cry out to God Most High,
To God, who fulfills His purpose for me. (Psalm 57:1-2)

READING

Slowly read the Scripture passage several times.

MEDITATION

Take some time to reflect on the words and phrases in the text.
Which words, phrases, or images speak most to you?

PRAYER

Offer the internalized passage back to God in the form of a personalized
prayer of adoration, confession, renewal, petition, intercession,
affirmation, or thanksgiving.

CONTEMPLATION

What word or image captures the spirit of the passage for you?

Take a few minutes to present yourself before God in silence and
yieldedness. When your mind wanders, center yourself by returning
to the spirit of the passage.

SCRIPTURE

Be exalted, O God, above the heavens;
Let Your glory be over all the earth.
I will praise You, O Lord, among the peoples;
I will sing to You among the nations.
For Your mercy reaches to the heavens,
And Your faithfulness reaches to the clouds.
Be exalted, O God, above the heavens;
Let Your glory be above all the earth. (Psalm 57:5,9-11)

READING

Slowly read the Scripture passage several times.

MEDITATION

Take some time to reflect on the words and phrases in the text.
Which words, phrases, or images speak most to you?

PRAYER

Offer the internalized passage back to God in the form of a personalized
prayer of adoration, confession, renewal, petition, intercession,
affirmation, or thanksgiving.

CONTEMPLATION

What word or image captures the spirit of the passage for you?

Take a few minutes to present yourself before God in silence and
yieldedness. When your mind wanders, center yourself by returning
to the spirit of the passage.

SCRIPTURE

I will sing of Your strength,
Yes, I will sing of Your mercy in the morning,
For You have been my stronghold,
My refuge in times of trouble.
To You, O my Strength, I will sing praises,
For God is my fortress, my loving God. (Psalm 59:16-17)

READING

Slowly read the Scripture passage several times.

MEDITATION

Take some time to reflect on the words and phrases in the text.
Which words, phrases, or images speak most to you?

PRAYER

Offer the internalized passage back to God in the form of a personalized
prayer of adoration, confession, renewal, petition, intercession,
affirmation, or thanksgiving.

CONTEMPLATION

What word or image captures the spirit of the passage for you?

Take a few minutes to present yourself before God in silence and
yieldedness. When your mind wanders, center yourself by returning
to the spirit of the passage.

SCRIPTURE

My soul silently waits for God alone;
My salvation comes from Him.
He alone is my rock and my salvation;
He is my stronghold; I will never be shaken. (Psalm 62:1-2)

READING

Slowly read the Scripture passage several times.

MEDITATION

Take some time to reflect on the words and phrases in the text.
Which words, phrases, or images speak most to you?

PRAYER

Offer the internalized passage back to God in the form of a personalized
prayer of adoration, confession, renewal, petition, intercession,
affirmation, or thanksgiving.

CONTEMPLATION

What word or image captures the spirit of the passage for you?

Take a few minutes to present yourself before God in silence and
yieldedness. When your mind wanders, center yourself by returning
to the spirit of the passage.

SCRIPTURE

Once God has spoken;
Twice I have heard this:
That power belongs to God,
And that You, O Lord, are loving.
For You reward each person according to what he has done.
(Psalm 62:11-12)

READING

Slowly read the Scripture passage several times.

MEDITATION

Take some time to reflect on the words and phrases in the text. Which words, phrases, or images speak most to you?

PRAYER

Offer the internalized passage back to God in the form of a personalized prayer of adoration, confession, renewal, petition, intercession, affirmation, or thanksgiving.

CONTEMPLATION

What word or image captures the spirit of the passage for you?

Take a few minutes to present yourself before God in silence and yieldedness. When your mind wanders, center yourself by returning to the spirit of the passage.

SCRIPTURE

You answer us with awesome deeds of righteousness,
O God of our salvation,
You who are the hope of all the ends of the earth
And of the farthest seas;
You formed the mountains by Your strength,
Having armed Yourself with power;
And You stilled the roaring of the seas,
The roaring of their waves,
And the tumult of the peoples. (Psalm 65:5-7)

READING

Slowly read the Scripture passage several times.

MEDITATION

Take some time to reflect on the words and phrases in the text.
Which words, phrases, or images speak most to you?

PRAYER

Offer the internalized passage back to God in the form of a personalized
prayer of adoration, confession, renewal, petition, intercession,
affirmation, or thanksgiving.

CONTEMPLATION

What word or image captures the spirit of the passage for you?

Take a few minutes to present yourself before God in silence and
yieldedness. When your mind wanders, center yourself by returning
to the spirit of the passage.

SCRIPTURE

Blessed be the Lord; day by day He bears our burdens,
The God of our salvation.
Our God is the God of salvation,
And to God the Lord belongs escape from death. (Psalm 68:19-20)

READING

Slowly read the Scripture passage several times.

MEDITATION

Take some time to reflect on the words and phrases in the text.
Which words, phrases, or images speak most to you?

PRAYER

Offer the internalized passage back to God in the form of a personalized
prayer of adoration, confession, renewal, petition, intercession,
affirmation, or thanksgiving.

CONTEMPLATION

What word or image captures the spirit of the passage for you?

Take a few minutes to present yourself before God in silence and
yieldedness. When your mind wanders, center yourself by returning
to the spirit of the passage.

SCRIPTURE

My mouth will tell of Your righteousness
And of Your salvation all day long,
Though I know not its measure.
I will come in the strength of the Lord God;
I will proclaim Your righteousness, Yours alone.
Since my youth, O God, You have taught me,
And to this day I declare Your wondrous deeds. (Psalm 71:15-17)

READING

Slowly read the Scripture passage several times.

MEDITATION

Take some time to reflect on the words and phrases in the text.
Which words, phrases, or images speak most to you?

PRAYER

Offer the internalized passage back to God in the form of a personalized
prayer of adoration, confession, renewal, petition, intercession,
affirmation, or thanksgiving.

CONTEMPLATION

What word or image captures the spirit of the passage for you?

Take a few minutes to present yourself before God in silence and
yieldedness. When your mind wanders, center yourself by returning
to the spirit of the passage.

SCRIPTURE

Your righteousness, O God, reaches to the heavens,
You who have done great things.
O God, who is like You? (Psalm 71:19)

READING

Slowly read the Scripture passage several times.

MEDITATION

Take some time to reflect on the words and phrases in the text.
Which words, phrases, or images speak most to you?

PRAYER

Offer the internalized passage back to God in the form of a personalized
prayer of adoration, confession, renewal, petition, intercession,
affirmation, or thanksgiving.

CONTEMPLATION

What word or image captures the spirit of the passage for you?

Take a few minutes to present yourself before God in silence and
yieldedness. When your mind wanders, center yourself by returning
to the spirit of the passage.

SCRIPTURE

Blessed be the Lord God, the God of Israel,
Who alone does wonderful things.
And blessed be His glorious name forever;
May the whole earth be filled with His glory.
Amen and Amen. (Psalm 72:18-19)

READING

Slowly read the Scripture passage several times.

MEDITATION

Take some time to reflect on the words and phrases in the text.
Which words, phrases, or images speak most to you?

PRAYER

Offer the internalized passage back to God in the form of a personalized
prayer of adoration, confession, renewal, petition, intercession,
affirmation, or thanksgiving.

CONTEMPLATION

What word or image captures the spirit of the passage for you?

Take a few minutes to present yourself before God in silence and
yieldedness. When your mind wanders, center yourself by returning
to the spirit of the passage.

SCRIPTURE

I am continually with You;
You hold me by my right hand.
You guide me with Your counsel,
And afterward You will take me to glory. (Psalm 73:23-24)

READING

Slowly read the Scripture passage several times.

MEDITATION

Take some time to reflect on the words and phrases in the text. Which words, phrases, or images speak most to you?

PRAYER

Offer the internalized passage back to God in the form of a personalized prayer of adoration, confession, renewal, petition, intercession, affirmation, or thanksgiving.

CONTEMPLATION

What word or image captures the spirit of the passage for you?

Take a few minutes to present yourself before God in silence and yieldedness. When your mind wanders, center yourself by returning to the spirit of the passage.

SCRIPTURE

I will remember the works of the Lord;
Surely, I will remember Your wonders of long ago.
I will meditate on all Your works
And consider all Your mighty deeds.
Your way, O God, is holy.
What god is so great as our God?
You are the God who works wonders;
You have revealed Your strength among the peoples.
You redeemed Your people with Your power,
The descendants of Jacob and Joseph. (Psalm 77:11-15)

READING

Slowly read the Scripture passage several times.

MEDITATION

Take some time to reflect on the words and phrases in the text.
Which words, phrases, or images speak most to you?

PRAYER

Offer the internalized passage back to God in the form of a personalized
prayer of adoration, confession, renewal, petition, intercession,
affirmation, or thanksgiving.

CONTEMPLATION

What word or image captures the spirit of the passage for you?

Take a few minutes to present yourself before God in silence and
yieldedness. When your mind wanders, center yourself by returning
to the spirit of the passage.

SCRIPTURE

Better is one day in Your courts than a thousand elsewhere;
I would rather be a doorkeeper in the house of my God
Than dwell in the tents of the wicked.
For the Lord God is a sun and shield;
The Lord will give grace and glory;
No good thing does He withhold from those who walk in integrity.
O Lord of hosts,
Blessed is the man who trusts in You! (Psalm 84:10-12)

READING

Slowly read the Scripture passage several times.

MEDITATION

Take some time to reflect on the words and phrases in the text.
Which words, phrases, or images speak most to you?

PRAYER

Offer the internalized passage back to God in the form of a personalized
prayer of adoration, confession, renewal, petition, intercession,
affirmation, or thanksgiving.

CONTEMPLATION

What word or image captures the spirit of the passage for you?

Take a few minutes to present yourself before God in silence and
yieldedness. When your mind wanders, center yourself by returning
to the spirit of the passage.

SCRIPTURE

Lovingkindness and truth have met together;
Righteousness and peace have kissed each other.
Truth shall spring forth from the earth,
And righteousness looks down from heaven. (Psalm 85:10-11)

READING

Slowly read the Scripture passage several times.

MEDITATION

Take some time to reflect on the words and phrases in the text.
Which words, phrases, or images speak most to you?

PRAYER

Offer the internalized passage back to God in the form of a personalized
prayer of adoration, confession, renewal, petition, intercession,
affirmation, or thanksgiving.

CONTEMPLATION

What word or image captures the spirit of the passage for you?

Take a few minutes to present yourself before God in silence and
yieldedness. When your mind wanders, center yourself by returning
to the spirit of the passage.

READING 48

SCRIPTURE

I will praise You, O Lord my God, with all my heart,
And I will glorify Your name forever.
For great is Your love toward me,
And You have delivered my soul from the depths of the grave.
(Psalm 86:12-13)

READING

Slowly read the Scripture passage several times.

MEDITATION

Take some time to reflect on the words and phrases in the text.
Which words, phrases, or images speak most to you?

PRAYER

Offer the internalized passage back to God in the form of a personalized
prayer of adoration, confession, renewal, petition, intercession,
affirmation, or thanksgiving.

CONTEMPLATION

What word or image captures the spirit of the passage for you?

Take a few minutes to present yourself before God in silence and
yieldedness. When your mind wanders, center yourself by returning
to the spirit of the passage.

SCRIPTURE

You, O Lord, are a compassionate and gracious God,
Slow to anger, and abounding in lovingkindness and truth. (Psalm 86:15)

READING

Slowly read the Scripture passage several times.

MEDITATION

Take some time to reflect on the words and phrases in the text.
Which words, phrases, or images speak most to you?

PRAYER

Offer the internalized passage back to God in the form of a personalized
prayer of adoration, confession, renewal, petition, intercession,
affirmation, or thanksgiving.

CONTEMPLATION

What word or image captures the spirit of the passage for you?

Take a few minutes to present yourself before God in silence and
yieldedness. When your mind wanders, center yourself by returning
to the spirit of the passage.

SCRIPTURE

I will sing of the mercies of the Lord forever;
With my mouth I will make Your faithfulness known through all generations.
I will declare that Your lovingkindness will be built up forever,
That You will establish Your faithfulness in the heavens.
And the heavens will praise Your wonders, O Lord,
Your faithfulness also in the assembly of the holy ones.
For who in the heavens can be compared with the Lord?
Who is like the Lord among the sons of the mighty?
God is greatly feared in the council of the holy ones
And more awesome than all who surround Him.
O Lord God of hosts, who is like You, O mighty Lord?
Your faithfulness also surrounds You. (Psalm 89:1-2,5-8)

READING

Slowly read the Scripture passage several times.

MEDITATION

Take some time to reflect on the words and phrases in the text.
Which words, phrases, or images speak most to you?

PRAYER

Offer the internalized passage back to God in the form of a personalized
prayer of adoration, confession, renewal, petition, intercession,
affirmation, or thanksgiving.

CONTEMPLATION

What word or image captures the spirit of the passage for you?

Take a few minutes to present yourself before God in silence and
yieldedness. When your mind wanders, center yourself by returning
to the spirit of the passage.

SCRIPTURE

Blessed are those who have learned to acclaim You,
Who walk in the light of Your presence, O Lord.
They rejoice in Your name all day long,
And they are exalted in Your righteousness. (Psalm 89:15-16)

READING

Slowly read the Scripture passage several times.

MEDITATION

Take some time to reflect on the words and phrases in the text.
Which words, phrases, or images speak most to you?

PRAYER

Offer the internalized passage back to God in the form of a personalized
prayer of adoration, confession, renewal, petition, intercession,
affirmation, or thanksgiving.

CONTEMPLATION

What word or image captures the spirit of the passage for you?

Take a few minutes to present yourself before God in silence and
yieldedness. When your mind wanders, center yourself by returning
to the spirit of the passage.

SCRIPTURE

Lord, You have been our dwelling place throughout all generations.
Before the mountains were born
Or You brought forth the earth and the world,
From everlasting to everlasting, You are God.
You turn men back into dust,
And say, "Return, O children of men."
For a thousand years in Your sight
Are like yesterday when it passes by
Or like a watch in the night. (Psalm 90:1-4)

READING

Slowly read the Scripture passage several times.

MEDITATION

Take some time to reflect on the words and phrases in the text.
Which words, phrases, or images speak most to you?

PRAYER

Offer the internalized passage back to God in the form of a personalized
prayer of adoration, confession, renewal, petition, intercession,
affirmation, or thanksgiving.

CONTEMPLATION

What word or image captures the spirit of the passage for you?

Take a few minutes to present yourself before God in silence and
yieldedness. When your mind wanders, center yourself by returning
to the spirit of the passage.

SCRIPTURE
He who dwells in the shelter of the Most High
Will rest in the shadow of the Almighty.
I will say of the Lord, "He is my refuge and my fortress,
My God, in whom I trust." (Psalm 91:1-2)

READING
Slowly read the Scripture passage several times.

MEDITATION
Take some time to reflect on the words and phrases in the text.
Which words, phrases, or images speak most to you?

PRAYER
Offer the internalized passage back to God in the form of a personalized
prayer of adoration, confession, renewal, petition, intercession,
affirmation, or thanksgiving.

CONTEMPLATION
What word or image captures the spirit of the passage for you?

Take a few minutes to present yourself before God in silence and
yieldedness. When your mind wanders, center yourself by returning
to the spirit of the passage.

SCRIPTURE

Because I love You, You will deliver me;
You will protect me, for I acknowledge Your name.
I will call upon You, and You will answer me;
You will be with me in trouble,
You will deliver me and honor me. (Psalm 91:14-15)

READING

Slowly read the Scripture passage several times.

MEDITATION

Take some time to reflect on the words and phrases in the text.
Which words, phrases, or images speak most to you?

PRAYER

Offer the internalized passage back to God in the form of a personalized
prayer of adoration, confession, renewal, petition, intercession,
affirmation, or thanksgiving.

CONTEMPLATION

What word or image captures the spirit of the passage for you?

Take a few minutes to present yourself before God in silence and
yieldedness. When your mind wanders, center yourself by returning
to the spirit of the passage.

SCRIPTURE

It is good to give thanks to the Lord
And to sing praises to Your name, O Most High,
To declare Your lovingkindness in the morning
And Your faithfulness at night. (Psalm 92:1-2)

READING

Slowly read the Scripture passage several times.

MEDITATION

Take some time to reflect on the words and phrases in the text.
Which words, phrases, or images speak most to you?

PRAYER

Offer the internalized passage back to God in the form of a personalized
prayer of adoration, confession, renewal, petition, intercession,
affirmation, or thanksgiving.

CONTEMPLATION

What word or image captures the spirit of the passage for you?

Take a few minutes to present yourself before God in silence and
yieldedness. When your mind wanders, center yourself by returning
to the spirit of the passage.

SCRIPTURE

The Lord reigns; He is clothed with majesty;
The Lord is robed in majesty and is armed with strength.
Indeed, the world is firmly established; it cannot be moved.
Your throne is established from of old;
You are from everlasting.
Your testimonies stand firm;
Holiness adorns Your house,
O Lord, forever. (Psalm 93:1-2,5)

READING

Slowly read the Scripture passage several times.

MEDITATION

Take some time to reflect on the words and phrases in the text.
Which words, phrases, or images speak most to you?

PRAYER

Offer the internalized passage back to God in the form of a personalized
prayer of adoration, confession, renewal, petition, intercession,
affirmation, or thanksgiving.

CONTEMPLATION

What word or image captures the spirit of the passage for you?

Take a few minutes to present yourself before God in silence and
yieldedness. When your mind wanders, center yourself by returning
to the spirit of the passage.

SCRIPTURE

The Lord is the great God,
The great King above all gods.
In His hand are the depths of the earth,
And the summits of the mountains are His also.
The sea is His, for He made it,
And His hands formed the dry land.
He is our God and we are the people of His pasture
And the sheep under His care. (Psalm 95:3-5,7)

READING

Slowly read the Scripture passage several times.

MEDITATION

Take some time to reflect on the words and phrases in the text.
Which words, phrases, or images speak most to you?

PRAYER

Offer the internalized passage back to God in the form of a personalized
prayer of adoration, confession, renewal, petition, intercession,
affirmation, or thanksgiving.

CONTEMPLATION

What word or image captures the spirit of the passage for you?

Take a few minutes to present yourself before God in silence and
yieldedness. When your mind wanders, center yourself by returning
to the spirit of the passage.

SCRIPTURE

O sing to the Lord a new song;
Sing to the Lord, all the earth.
Sing to the Lord, bless His name;
Proclaim the good news of His salvation day after day.
Declare His glory among the nations,
His marvelous works among all people. (Psalm 96:1-3)

READING

Slowly read the Scripture passage several times.

MEDITATION

Take some time to reflect on the words and phrases in the text.
Which words, phrases, or images speak most to you?

PRAYER

Offer the internalized passage back to God in the form of a personalized
prayer of adoration, confession, renewal, petition, intercession,
affirmation, or thanksgiving.

CONTEMPLATION

What word or image captures the spirit of the passage for you?

Take a few minutes to present yourself before God in silence and
yieldedness. When your mind wanders, center yourself by returning
to the spirit of the passage.

SCRIPTURE

Great is the Lord and most worthy of praise;
He is to be feared above all gods.
For all the gods of the nations are idols,
But the Lord made the heavens.
Splendor and majesty are before Him;
Strength and beauty are in His sanctuary.
I will ascribe to the Lord glory and strength.
I will ascribe to the Lord the glory due His name
And worship the Lord in the beauty of holiness. (Psalm 96:4-8)

READING

Slowly read the Scripture passage several times.

MEDITATION

Take some time to reflect on the words and phrases in the text.
Which words, phrases, or images speak most to you?

PRAYER

Offer the internalized passage back to God in the form of a personalized
prayer of adoration, confession, renewal, petition, intercession,
affirmation, or thanksgiving.

CONTEMPLATION

What word or image captures the spirit of the passage for you?

Take a few minutes to present yourself before God in silence and
yieldedness. When your mind wanders, center yourself by returning
to the spirit of the passage.

SCRIPTURE

Let those who love the Lord hate evil.
He preserves the souls of His saints
And delivers them from the hand of the wicked.
Light is sown for the righteous
And gladness for the upright in heart. (Psalm 97:10-11)

READING

Slowly read the Scripture passage several times.

MEDITATION

Take some time to reflect on the words and phrases in the text.
Which words, phrases, or images speak most to you?

PRAYER

Offer the internalized passage back to God in the form of a personalized
prayer of adoration, confession, renewal, petition, intercession,
affirmation, or thanksgiving.

CONTEMPLATION

What word or image captures the spirit of the passage for you?

Take a few minutes to present yourself before God in silence and
yieldedness. When your mind wanders, center yourself by returning
to the spirit of the passage.

SCRIPTURE

Shout joyfully to the Lord, all the earth.
Worship the Lord with gladness;
Come before Him with joyful singing.
The Lord, He is God.
It is He who made us, and not we ourselves;
We are His people and the sheep of His pasture. (Psalm 100:1-3)

READING

Slowly read the Scripture passage several times.

MEDITATION

Take some time to reflect on the words and phrases in the text.
Which words, phrases, or images speak most to you?

PRAYER

Offer the internalized passage back to God in the form of a personalized
prayer of adoration, confession, renewal, petition, intercession,
affirmation, or thanksgiving.

CONTEMPLATION

What word or image captures the spirit of the passage for you?

Take a few minutes to present yourself before God in silence and
yieldedness. When your mind wanders, center yourself by returning
to the spirit of the passage.

SCRIPTURE

I will enter the Lord's gates with thanksgiving
And His courts with praise;
I will give thanks to Him and bless His name.
For the Lord is good
And His lovingkindness endures forever;
His faithfulness continues through all generations. (Psalm 100:4-5)

READING

Slowly read the Scripture passage several times.

MEDITATION

Take some time to reflect on the words and phrases in the text.
Which words, phrases, or images speak most to you?

PRAYER

Offer the internalized passage back to God in the form of a personalized
prayer of adoration, confession, renewal, petition, intercession,
affirmation, or thanksgiving.

CONTEMPLATION

What word or image captures the spirit of the passage for you?

Take a few minutes to present yourself before God in silence and
yieldedness. When your mind wanders, center yourself by returning
to the spirit of the passage.

SCRIPTURE

My days are like a lengthened shadow,
And I wither away like grass.
But You, O Lord, will endure forever,
And the remembrance of Your name to all generations.
Of old, You laid the foundations of the earth,
And the heavens are the work of Your hands.
They will perish, but You will endure;
They will all wear out like a garment.
Like clothing, You will change them, and they will be discarded.
But You are the same,
And Your years will have no end. (Psalm 102:11-12,25-27)

READING

Slowly read the Scripture passage several times.

MEDITATION

Take some time to reflect on the words and phrases in the text.
Which words, phrases, or images speak most to you?

PRAYER

Offer the internalized passage back to God in the form of a personalized
prayer of adoration, confession, renewal, petition, intercession,
affirmation, or thanksgiving.

CONTEMPLATION

What word or image captures the spirit of the passage for you?

Take a few minutes to present yourself before God in silence and
yieldedness. When your mind wanders, center yourself by returning
to the spirit of the passage.

SCRIPTURE

Bless the Lord, O my soul;
And all that is within me, bless His holy name.
Bless the Lord, O my soul,
And forget not all His benefits;
Who forgives all your iniquities
And heals all your diseases;
Who redeems your life from the pit
And crowns you with love and compassion;
Who satisfies your desires with good things,
So that your youth is renewed like the eagle's. (Psalm 103:1-5)

READING

Slowly read the Scripture passage several times.

MEDITATION

Take some time to reflect on the words and phrases in the text.
Which words, phrases, or images speak most to you?

PRAYER

Offer the internalized passage back to God in the form of a personalized
prayer of adoration, confession, renewal, petition, intercession,
affirmation, or thanksgiving.

CONTEMPLATION

What word or image captures the spirit of the passage for you?

Take a few minutes to present yourself before God in silence and
yieldedness. When your mind wanders, center yourself by returning
to the spirit of the passage.

SCRIPTURE

The Lord executes righteousness
And justice for all who are oppressed.
The Lord is compassionate and gracious,
Slow to anger, and abounding in lovingkindness. (Psalm 103:6,8)

READING

Slowly read the Scripture passage several times.

MEDITATION

Take some time to reflect on the words and phrases in the text.
Which words, phrases, or images speak most to you?

PRAYER

Offer the internalized passage back to God in the form of a personalized
prayer of adoration, confession, renewal, petition, intercession,
affirmation, or thanksgiving.

CONTEMPLATION

What word or image captures the spirit of the passage for you?

Take a few minutes to present yourself before God in silence and
yieldedness. When your mind wanders, center yourself by returning
to the spirit of the passage.

SCRIPTURE

Bless the Lord, O my soul.
O Lord, my God, You are very great;
You are clothed with splendor and majesty. (Psalm 104:1)

READING

Slowly read the Scripture passage several times.

MEDITATION

Take some time to reflect on the words and phrases in the text.
Which words, phrases, or images speak most to you?

PRAYER

Offer the internalized passage back to God in the form of a personalized
prayer of adoration, confession, renewal, petition, intercession,
affirmation, or thanksgiving.

CONTEMPLATION

What word or image captures the spirit of the passage for you?

Take a few minutes to present yourself before God in silence and
yieldedness. When your mind wanders, center yourself by returning
to the spirit of the passage.

SCRIPTURE

The Lord covers Himself in light as with a garment;
He stretches out the heavens like a tent curtain
And lays the beams of His upper chambers in the waters.
He makes the clouds His chariot, and walks on the wings of the wind.
He makes the winds His messengers, flames of fire His servants.
He set the earth on its foundations, so that it can never be moved.
You covered it with the deep as with a garment;
The waters stood above the mountains.
At Your rebuke the waters fled;
At the sound of Your thunder they hurried away.
They flowed over the mountains, and went down into the valleys
To the place You assigned for them.
You set a boundary they cannot cross,
That they will not return to cover the earth.
O Lord, how manifold are Your works!
In wisdom You made them all; the earth is full of Your possessions.
(Psalm 104:2-9,24)

READING
Slowly read the Scripture passage several times.

MEDITATION
Take some time to reflect on the words and phrases in the text.
Which words, phrases, or images speak most to you?

PRAYER
Offer the internalized passage back to God in the form of a personalized
prayer of adoration, confession, renewal, petition, intercession,
affirmation, or thanksgiving.

CONTEMPLATION
What word or image captures the spirit of the passage for you?

Take a few minutes to present yourself before God in silence and
yieldedness. When your mind wanders, center yourself by returning
to the spirit of the passage.

ADING 68

SCRIPTURE

I will give thanks to the Lord, for He is good;
His lovingkindness endures forever.
I will give thanks to the Lord for His unfailing love
And His wonderful acts to the children of men,
For He satisfies the thirsty soul
And fills the hungry soul with good things. (Psalm 107:1,8-9)

READING

Slowly read the Scripture passage several times.

MEDITATION

Take some time to reflect on the words and phrases in the text.
Which words, phrases, or images speak most to you?

PRAYER

Offer the internalized passage back to God in the form of a personalized
prayer of adoration, confession, renewal, petition, intercession,
affirmation, or thanksgiving.

CONTEMPLATION

What word or image captures the spirit of the passage for you?

Take a few minutes to present yourself before God in silence and
yieldedness. When your mind wanders, center yourself by returning
to the spirit of the passage.

SCRIPTURE

Great are the works of the Lord;
They are pondered by all who delight in them.
Splendid and majestic is His work,
And His righteousness endures forever.
He has caused His wonderful acts to be remembered;
The Lord is gracious and compassionate. (Psalm 111:2-4)

READING

Slowly read the Scripture passage several times.

MEDITATION

Take some time to reflect on the words and phrases in the text.
Which words, phrases, or images speak most to you?

PRAYER

Offer the internalized passage back to God in the form of a personalized
prayer of adoration, confession, renewal, petition, intercession,
affirmation, or thanksgiving.

CONTEMPLATION

What word or image captures the spirit of the passage for you?

Take a few minutes to present yourself before God in silence and
yieldedness. When your mind wanders, center yourself by returning
to the spirit of the passage.

SCRIPTURE

The fear of the Lord is the beginning of wisdom;
All who practice His commandments have a good understanding.
His praise endures forever. (Psalm 111:10)

READING

Slowly read the Scripture passage several times.

MEDITATION

Take some time to reflect on the words and phrases in the text.
Which words, phrases, or images speak most to you?

PRAYER

Offer the internalized passage back to God in the form of a personalized
prayer of adoration, confession, renewal, petition, intercession,
affirmation, or thanksgiving.

CONTEMPLATION

What word or image captures the spirit of the passage for you?

Take a few minutes to present yourself before God in silence and
yieldedness. When your mind wanders, center yourself by returning
to the spirit of the passage.

SCRIPTURE

Praise the Lord!
Praise, O servants of the Lord,
Praise the name of the Lord.
Blessed be the name of the Lord
Both now and forever.
From the rising of the sun to its setting,
The name of the Lord is to be praised.
The Lord is high above all nations,
His glory above the heavens.
Who is like the Lord our God,
The One who is enthroned on high,
Who humbles Himself to behold
The things that are in the heavens and in the earth? (Psalm 113:1-6)

READING

Slowly read the Scripture passage several times.

MEDITATION

Take some time to reflect on the words and phrases in the text.
Which words, phrases, or images speak most to you?

PRAYER

Offer the internalized passage back to God in the form of a personalized
prayer of adoration, confession, renewal, petition, intercession,
affirmation, or thanksgiving.

CONTEMPLATION

What word or image captures the spirit of the passage for you?

Take a few minutes to present yourself before God in silence and
yieldedness. When your mind wanders, center yourself by returning
to the spirit of the passage.

SCRIPTURE

You are my God, and I will give thanks to You;
You are my God, and I will exalt You.
I will give thanks to the Lord, for He is good;
His loyal love endures forever. (Psalm 118:28-29)

READING

Slowly read the Scripture passage several times.

MEDITATION

Take some time to reflect on the words and phrases in the text.
Which words, phrases, or images speak most to you?

PRAYER

Offer the internalized passage back to God in the form of a personalized
prayer of adoration, confession, renewal, petition, intercession,
affirmation, or thanksgiving.

CONTEMPLATION

What word or image captures the spirit of the passage for you?

Take a few minutes to present yourself before God in silence and
yieldedness. When your mind wanders, center yourself by returning
to the spirit of the passage.

SCRIPTURE

Blessed are those whose ways are blameless,
Who walk in the law of the Lord.
Blessed are those who keep His testimonies
And seek Him with all their heart. (Psalm 119:1-2)

READING

Slowly read the Scripture passage several times.

MEDITATION

Take some time to reflect on the words and phrases in the text.
Which words, phrases, or images speak most to you?

PRAYER

Offer the internalized passage back to God in the form of a personalized
prayer of adoration, confession, renewal, petition, intercession,
affirmation, or thanksgiving.

CONTEMPLATION

What word or image captures the spirit of the passage for you?

Take a few minutes to present yourself before God in silence and
yieldedness. When your mind wanders, center yourself by returning
to the spirit of the passage.

SCRIPTURE

Your word is settled in heaven forever, O Lord.
Your faithfulness continues through all generations;
You established the earth, and it stands.
They continue to this day according to Your ordinances,
For all things serve You. (Psalm 119:89-91)

READING

Slowly read the Scripture passage several times.

MEDITATION

Take some time to reflect on the words and phrases in the text.
Which words, phrases, or images speak most to you?

PRAYER

Offer the internalized passage back to God in the form of a personalized
prayer of adoration, confession, renewal, petition, intercession,
affirmation, or thanksgiving.

CONTEMPLATION

What word or image captures the spirit of the passage for you?

Take a few minutes to present yourself before God in silence and
yieldedness. When your mind wanders, center yourself by returning
to the spirit of the passage.

SCRIPTURE

Your word is a lamp to my feet
And a light to my path.
I have inclined my heart to perform Your statutes
To the very end. (Psalm 119:105,112)

READING

Slowly read the Scripture passage several times.

MEDITATION

Take some time to reflect on the words and phrases in the text.
Which words, phrases, or images speak most to you?

PRAYER

Offer the internalized passage back to God in the form of a personalized
prayer of adoration, confession, renewal, petition, intercession,
affirmation, or thanksgiving.

CONTEMPLATION

What word or image captures the spirit of the passage for you?

Take a few minutes to present yourself before God in silence and
yieldedness. When your mind wanders, center yourself by returning
to the spirit of the passage.

SCRIPTURE

I rejoice at Your word, as one who finds great spoil.
I hate and abhor falsehood, but I love Your law.
Great peace have they who love Your law,
And nothing causes them to stumble.
O Lord, I hope for Your salvation, and I follow Your commands.
My soul keeps Your testimonies, for I love them greatly.
I keep Your precepts and Your testimonies,
For all my ways are known to You. (Psalm 119:162-163,165-168)

READING

Slowly read the Scripture passage several times.

MEDITATION

Take some time to reflect on the words and phrases in the text.
Which words, phrases, or images speak most to you?

PRAYER

Offer the internalized passage back to God in the form of a personalized
prayer of adoration, confession, renewal, petition, intercession,
affirmation, or thanksgiving.

CONTEMPLATION

What word or image captures the spirit of the passage for you?

Take a few minutes to present yourself before God in silence and
yieldedness. When your mind wanders, center yourself by returning to
the spirit of the passage.

SCRIPTURE

I lift up my eyes to the hills—
Where does my help come from?
My help comes from the Lord,
Who made heaven and earth.
He will not allow my foot to slip;
He who watches over me will not slumber.
The Lord is my keeper;
The Lord is my shade at my right hand.
The sun will not harm me by day,
Nor the moon by night. (Psalm 121:1-3,5-6)

READING

Slowly read the Scripture passage several times.

MEDITATION

Take some time to reflect on the words and phrases in the text.
Which words, phrases, or images speak most to you?

PRAYER

Offer the internalized passage back to God in the form of a personalized
prayer of adoration, confession, renewal, petition, intercession,
affirmation, or thanksgiving.

CONTEMPLATION

What word or image captures the spirit of the passage for you?

Take a few minutes to present yourself before God in silence and
yieldedness. When your mind wanders, center yourself by returning
to the spirit of the passage.

SCRIPTURE

I lift up my eyes to You,
To You who dwell in heaven.
As the eyes of servants look to the hand of their master,
As the eyes of a maid look to the hand of her mistress,
So my eyes look to the Lord my God,
Until He shows me His mercy. (Psalm 123:1-2)

READING

Slowly read the Scripture passage several times.

MEDITATION

Take some time to reflect on the words and phrases in the text.
Which words, phrases, or images speak most to you?

PRAYER

Offer the internalized passage back to God in the form of a personalized
prayer of adoration, confession, renewal, petition, intercession,
affirmation, or thanksgiving.

CONTEMPLATION

What word or image captures the spirit of the passage for you?

Take a few minutes to present yourself before God in silence and
yieldedness. When your mind wanders, center yourself by returning
to the spirit of the passage.

SCRIPTURE

I know that the Lord is great,
And that our Lord is above all gods.
Whatever the Lord pleases, He does,
In the heavens and on the earth,
In the seas and all their depths. (Psalm 135:5-6)

READING

Slowly read the Scripture passage several times.

MEDITATION

Take some time to reflect on the words and phrases in the text.
Which words, phrases, or images speak most to you?

PRAYER

Offer the internalized passage back to God in the form of a personalized
prayer of adoration, confession, renewal, petition, intercession,
affirmation, or thanksgiving.

CONTEMPLATION

What word or image captures the spirit of the passage for you?

Take a few minutes to present yourself before God in silence and
yieldedness. When your mind wanders, center yourself by returning
to the spirit of the passage.

SCRIPTURE

Though I walk in the midst of trouble, You will revive me;
You will stretch out Your hand against the anger of my foes,
And Your right hand will save me.
The Lord will perfect His work in me;
Your mercy, O Lord, endures forever;
You will not abandon the works of Your hands. (Psalm 138:7-8)

READING

Slowly read the Scripture passage several times.

MEDITATION

Take some time to reflect on the words and phrases in the text.
Which words, phrases, or images speak most to you?

PRAYER

Offer the internalized passage back to God in the form of a personalized
prayer of adoration, confession, renewal, petition, intercession,
affirmation, or thanksgiving.

CONTEMPLATION

What word or image captures the spirit of the passage for you?

Take a few minutes to present yourself before God in silence and
yieldedness. When your mind wanders, center yourself by returning
to the spirit of the passage.

SCRIPTURE

O Lord, You have searched me and You know me.
You know when I sit down and when I rise up;
You understand my thoughts from afar.
You scrutinize my path and my lying down
And are acquainted with all my ways.
Before a word is on my tongue,
O Lord, You know it completely.
You have enclosed me behind and before,
And laid Your hand upon me.
Such knowledge is too wonderful for me;
It is too lofty for me to attain. (Psalm 139:1-6)

READING

Slowly read the Scripture passage several times.

MEDITATION

Take some time to reflect on the words and phrases in the text.
Which words, phrases, or images speak most to you?

PRAYER

Offer the internalized passage back to God in the form of a personalized
prayer of adoration, confession, renewal, petition, intercession,
affirmation, or thanksgiving.

CONTEMPLATION

What word or image captures the spirit of the passage for you?

Take a few minutes to present yourself before God in silence and
yieldedness. When your mind wanders, center yourself by returning
to the spirit of the passage.

SCRIPTURE

You formed my inward parts;
You wove me together in my mother's womb.
I thank You because I am fearfully and wonderfully made;
Your works are wonderful,
And my soul knows it full well.
My frame was not hidden from You
When I was made in secret
And skillfully wrought in the depths of the earth.
Your eyes saw my embryo,
And all the days ordained for me
Were written in Your book
Before one of them came to be. (Psalm 139:13-16)

READING

Slowly read the Scripture passage several times.

MEDITATION

Take some time to reflect on the words and phrases in the text.
Which words, phrases, or images speak most to you?

PRAYER

Offer the internalized passage back to God in the form of a personalized
prayer of adoration, confession, renewal, petition, intercession,
affirmation, or thanksgiving.

CONTEMPLATION

What word or image captures the spirit of the passage for you?

Take a few minutes to present yourself before God in silence and
yieldedness. When your mind wanders, center yourself by returning
to the spirit of the passage.

SCRIPTURE

How precious are Your thoughts to me, O God!
How vast is the sum of them!
If I should count them, they would outnumber the grains of sand.
When I awake, I am still with You. (Psalm 139:17-18)

READING

Slowly read the Scripture passage several times.

MEDITATION

Take some time to reflect on the words and phrases in the text.
Which words, phrases, or images speak most to you?

PRAYER

Offer the internalized passage back to God in the form of a personalized
prayer of adoration, confession, renewal, petition, intercession,
affirmation, or thanksgiving.

CONTEMPLATION

What word or image captures the spirit of the passage for you?

Take a few minutes to present yourself before God in silence and
yieldedness. When your mind wanders, center yourself by returning
to the spirit of the passage.

SCRIPTURE

Search me, O God, and know my heart;
Try me and know my anxious thoughts,
And see if there is any wicked way in me,
And lead me in the way everlasting. (Psalm 139:23-24)

READING

Slowly read the Scripture passage several times.

MEDITATION

Take some time to reflect on the words and phrases in the text.
Which words, phrases, or images speak most to you?

PRAYER

Offer the internalized passage back to God in the form of a personalized
prayer of adoration, confession, renewal, petition, intercession,
affirmation, or thanksgiving.

CONTEMPLATION

What word or image captures the spirit of the passage for you?

Take a few minutes to present yourself before God in silence and
yieldedness. When your mind wanders, center yourself by returning
to the spirit of the passage.

SCRIPTURE

I will exalt You, my God and King;
I will bless Your name for ever and ever.
Every day I will bless You,
And I will praise Your name for ever and ever.
Great is the Lord and most worthy of praise;
His greatness is unsearchable. (Psalm 145:1-3)

READING

Slowly read the Scripture passage several times.

MEDITATION

Take some time to reflect on the words and phrases in the text.
Which words, phrases, or images speak most to you?

PRAYER

Offer the internalized passage back to God in the form of a personalized
prayer of adoration, confession, renewal, petition, intercession,
affirmation, or thanksgiving.

CONTEMPLATION

What word or image captures the spirit of the passage for you?

Take a few minutes to present yourself before God in silence and
yieldedness. When your mind wanders, center yourself by returning
to the spirit of the passage.

SCRIPTURE

One generation shall praise Your works to another,
And shall declare Your mighty acts.
I will meditate on the glorious splendor of Your majesty
And on Your wonderful works.
Men shall speak of the might of Your awesome works,
And I will proclaim Your great deeds. (Psalm 145:4-6)

READING

Slowly read the Scripture passage several times.

MEDITATION

Take some time to reflect on the words and phrases in the text.
Which words, phrases, or images speak most to you?

PRAYER

Offer the internalized passage back to God in the form of a personalized prayer of adoration, confession, renewal, petition, intercession, affirmation, or thanksgiving.

CONTEMPLATION

What word or image captures the spirit of the passage for you?

Take a few minutes to present yourself before God in silence and yieldedness. When your mind wanders, center yourself by returning to the spirit of the passage.

SCRIPTURE

I will express the memory of Your abundant goodness
And joyfully sing of Your righteousness.
The Lord is gracious and compassionate,
Slow to anger, and great in lovingkindness.
The Lord is good to all,
And His tender mercies are over all His works. (Psalm 145:7-9)

READING

Slowly read the Scripture passage several times.

MEDITATION

Take some time to reflect on the words and phrases in the text.
Which words, phrases, or images speak most to you?

PRAYER

Offer the internalized passage back to God in the form of a personalized
prayer of adoration, confession, renewal, petition, intercession,
affirmation, or thanksgiving.

CONTEMPLATION

What word or image captures the spirit of the passage for you?

Take a few minutes to present yourself before God in silence and
yieldedness. When your mind wanders, center yourself by returning
to the spirit of the passage.

SCRIPTURE

The Lord upholds all who fall
And lifts up all who are bowed down.
The eyes of all look to You,
And You give them their food at the proper time.
You open Your hand
And satisfy the desire of every living thing. (Psalm 145:14-16)

READING

Slowly read the Scripture passage several times.

MEDITATION

Take some time to reflect on the words and phrases in the text.
Which words, phrases, or images speak most to you?

PRAYER

Offer the internalized passage back to God in the form of a personalized
prayer of adoration, confession, renewal, petition, intercession,
affirmation, or thanksgiving.

CONTEMPLATION

What word or image captures the spirit of the passage for you?

Take a few minutes to present yourself before God in silence and
yieldedness. When your mind wanders, center yourself by returning
to the spirit of the passage.

SCRIPTURE

The Lord is near to all who call upon Him,
To all who call upon Him in truth.
He fulfills the desire of those who fear Him;
He hears their cry and saves them.
The Lord preserves all who love Him,
But all the wicked He will destroy. (Psalm 145:18-20)

READING

Slowly read the Scripture passage several times.

MEDITATION

Take some time to reflect on the words and phrases in the text.
Which words, phrases, or images speak most to you?

PRAYER

Offer the internalized passage back to God in the form of a personalized
prayer of adoration, confession, renewal, petition, intercession,
affirmation, or thanksgiving.

CONTEMPLATION

What word or image captures the spirit of the passage for you?

Take a few minutes to present yourself before God in silence and
yieldedness. When your mind wanders, center yourself by returning
to the spirit of the passage.

SCRIPTURE

The Lord takes pleasure in those who fear Him,
Who put their hope in His unfailing love. (Psalm 147:11)

READING

Slowly read the Scripture passage several times.

MEDITATION

Take some time to reflect on the words and phrases in the text.
Which words, phrases, or images speak most to you?

PRAYER

Offer the internalized passage back to God in the form of a personalized
prayer of adoration, confession, renewal, petition, intercession,
affirmation, or thanksgiving.

CONTEMPLATION

What word or image captures the spirit of the passage for you?

Take a few minutes to present yourself before God in silence and yieldedness. When your mind wanders, center yourself by returning to the
spirit of the passage.

WHERE TO GO FROM HERE

I trust that this ninety-day process has been meaningful and spiritually nourishing for you. Now that you have completed *The Psalms: A Journal,* you should go back and read through the comments and prayers you have recorded. As you do this, be sure to mark the journal entries that strongly resonate with your spirit.

As I mentioned at the end of the introduction, it would be especially helpful for you to go through this process a second time and visit each of these passages once again. You will discover new things in the Scripture texts that did not see the first time through. Use a different color of ink for your journal comments each time you revisit a passage.

I also encourage you to use the other journals in this *Reflections* series. *Sacred Readings: A Journal* presents ninety Scripture texts from Numbers through Revelation that are particularly well-suited to the process of sacred reading. These texts range from one to several verses, and they are arranged in biblical sequence to attune you to the flow of progressive revelation.

Historic Creeds: A Journal moves through three historic creeds of the faith (the Apostles' Creed, the Nicene Creed, and the Athanasian Creed) and relates each element of these creeds to a Scripture text for sacred reading.

The Trinity: A Journal is designed to take you on a meditative journey through each of the three Persons of the divine Trinity by guiding you through thirty passages on the Father, thirty passages on the Son, and thirty passages on the Holy Spirit.

ABOUT THE AUTHOR

DR. KENNETH BOA is the president of Reflections Ministries. He has authored many books including *Pursuing Wisdom* and *The Art of Living Well* (both NavPress) and is a contributing editor to the *Open Bible,* the *Promise Keeper's Men's Study Bible,* and the *Leadership Bible.* Dr. Boa earned a bachelor's degree from Case Institute of Technology, a master's degree in theology from Dallas Theological Seminary, and doctoral degrees from both New York University and the University of Oxford. He resides in Atlanta, Georgia.

Kenneth Boa writes a free monthly teaching letter called *Reflections.* If you would like to be on the mailing list, call: 800-DRAW NEAR (800-372-9632).

COME FACE TO FACE WITH GOD

The Trinity

Through contemplative reading you'll examine ninety passages that will give you a deeper knowledge of each of the Persons of the Trinity. Get to know God—Father, Son, and Spirit—intimately.

The Trinity (Kenneth Boa) $10

Sacred Readings

Are you seeking meaningful time with God? This journal will help you intensify your relationship with Him as you study the sacred Scriptures of the faith.

Sacred Readings (Kenneth Boa) $10

Historic Creeds

A number of historic statements, including the Apostles' Creed, will help you develop a better understanding of the truths upon which Christ's church was built.

Historic Creeds (Kenneth Boa) $10

Get your copies today at your local bookstore, visit our website at www.navpress.com, or call (800) 366-7788 and ask for offer **#6120** or a FREE catalog of NavPress products.

NAVPRESS
BRINGING TRUTH TO LIFE
w w w . n a v p r e s s . c o m

Prices subject to change.